Take the **CANQUIZ**
Test Your Canadian Trivia Knowledge!

CANQUIZ

KEY PORTER ≈ BOOKS

Alastair Sweeny

National Library of Canada Cataloguing in Publication Data

Sweeny, Alastair
    CanQuiz / Alastair Sweeny.

ISBN 1-55263-415-9

    1. Canada—Miscellanea. I. Title.

FC61.S94 2002   971   C2002-901322-4
F1008.S94 2002

ONTARIO ARTS COUNCIL
CONSEIL DES ARTS DE L'ONTARIO

The publisher gratefully acknowledges the support of the Canada Council for the Arts and the Ontario Arts
Council for its publishing program.

We acknowledge the financial support of the Government of Canada through the Book Publishing Industry
Development Program (BPIDP) for our publishing activities.

Key Porter Books Limited
70 The Esplanade
Toronto, Ontario
Canada M5E 1R2

www.keyporter.com

The following are acknowledged for providing many of the photos and images in this book: National Archives of
Canada (NAC), National Library of Canada (NLC), Canada Post, Canadian Press (CP), Library of Congress, and
National Aeronautics & Space Administration (NASA).
Design and electronic formatting: Lightfoot Art & Design Inc.

Printed and bound in Canada

02 03 04 05 06 6 5 4 3 2 1

Contents

Acknowledgements

Thanks to all who helped whip these quizzes
into shape, and especially Gaetane Lemay,
Susan Brown, Lorne Rubenstein, Richard Evers,
and at Key Porter, Clare McKeon and Peter
Atwood.

If you're a purchaser of this book,
you can get three months, free access
to CANQUIZ online. For details,
please go to www.canquiz.ca/trial.html.
Your password is **"keyporter"** in lowercase
type. CanQuiz online is a project of
The Canada Channel www.canchan.ca.
For further information, please contact
info@canquiz.ca.

To the Reader:

When I was asked in 1985 to help research the history of the Hudson's Bay Company, I was surprised—but not shocked—that what was needed most, I was told, were "quirky details," odd snippets that added character and zest to a story.

The country Canada is chock full of quirky details, as quirky as anywhere in the world, and many of our quirks make fine quiz fodder, as you will see.

Let's take inventors, for instance. Most of us walk around burdened with such bland trivialities as "Edison invented the light bulb," "Abner Doubleday invented baseball" and "Marconi invented radio." This is bothersome nonsense, and it's time we told the world that it was temperamental Canadian tinkerers who made all these things work.

Young Canucks should be taught at an early age that this is the land that invented practically everything: from the light bulb, radio, TV, hockey, baseball, basketball, football, oil refining, fibre optics, the synthesizer, insulin and time (standard); to comedy, Hollywood, computer animation, Java, canola, the credit union, the electric stove, the washing machine, the snow blower, the pacemaker and the Ski-doo—to name but a small few.

Other nations may brag, but this is the land that is home to the world's largest shopping mall, the world's longest bridge over water, the world's tallest building, the world's largest paperback seller, the world's largest man, and even the world's largest frog. Not to mention the oldest rock, the largest bay, the broadest strait, the strongest currents and the highest tides in the world.

It's not always easy correcting our mistaken assumptions, but quizzes are a great place to start, because we learn best by making mistakes, or by being surprised. There's a lot of genuinely startling info in the pages ahead that you'll never see on Alex Trebek's quiz show—even if he was born July 22, 1940, in Sudbury, Ontario, and got his start on CBC's "Reach for the Top."

Want to know more? Read on, and enjoy.

Alastair Sweeny

History?

Canada Discovered

Canada Faces Disaster

Canada at War

Canada Invents

Canada Firsts and Bests

CANADA DISCOVERED

1 What was wampum used for by early First Nations tribes?

2 Where was the first permanent European settlement in Canada?

3 Did Great Britain ever consider negotiating with France to give up Canada in exchange for a tiny tropical island only 1,706 square kilometres in size, about one-quarter the size of Prince Edward Island?

4 Where did the word "Canada" come from?

5 In the first half of the nineteenth century, an entire group of aboriginal peoples was wiped out by war and disease. Who were these people?

6 During the American Revolution, Mohawk leader Thayendanega led a large number of the Six Nations people into Canada from the emerging United States. What was he called in English?

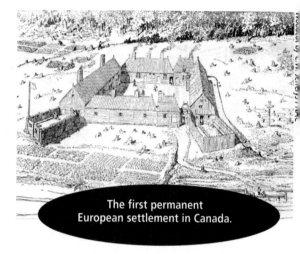

The first permanent European settlement in Canada.

7 Tecumseh, a Shawnee from US territory, fled north to Canada to avoid persecution by American troops. Isaac Brock made him a general and military leader of those who escaped to Canada with him. In the War of 1812, his forces captured what large fort in the United States?

8 Which 1873 massacre of Canadian Indians by American wolf hunters in what is now southeastern Alberta jump-started the founding of the North West Mounted Police?
A. Seven Oaks
B. Wounded Knee
C. Cypress Hills
D. Frog Lake

9 Which Canadian First Nations people discovered Europe?

10 According to Chinese records, the west coast of North America was discovered by Chinese Imperial astronomers. True?

11 Mi'kmaq legend speaks of bearded visitors with red hair and green eyes who showed the Mi'kmaq people how to fish with nets. Some Scots claim that an Orkney Islands captain sailed with 12 ships and 300 men, landing in Guysborough, Nova Scotia, on June 12, 1398. Who was this Scottish adventurer?

12 The "Flateyjarbok" and "Hauk's Book," two medieval Icelandic narratives, both tell of a Norse merchant who sailed to the New World. Who was the first Norse explorer to reach Canada?

13 In 1997 Newfoundland celebrated the 500th anniversary of the first discovery of the island by Europeans since the Vikings. Who was the discoverer, and where did he come from?

14 Why did one early map place a Portuguese flag over Canada?

15 When and where was the first French settlement in Canada?

16 Which king sent French explorer Jacques Cartier on a voyage to discover a route to the Orient through North America, and to discover great quantities of gold and other riches?
A. Louis IX
B. Henry VIII
C. François I
D. Louis XIII

CANADA DISCOVERED

17 In 1598 the Marquis de la Roche, French lieutenant-general of Canada, tried to establish a colony on Sable Island off Nova Scotia with what colonists?

18 When and where was the first English settlement in Canada?

The Canadian west is opened to European trade.

19 What Quebec soldier, farmer, fur trader and explorer is credited with opening up the whole western country to European trade?

20 François de Varennes de La Vérendrye is credited as being the first European to discover this lake, which is the 13th largest in the world.

21 This explorer, born in Trois Rivières in 1685, spent much of his life attempting to discover the western sea and was the first European to explore the Great Lakes and visit the site of Toronto.

22 Who was the first explorer to cross Canada by land, arriving at the Pacific Ocean in 1793?

23 Hudson's Bay Company employee Henry Kelsey, on a trade trip from York Factory on Hudson Bay, was the first European to visit which modern-day western province?

24 When was the term "Canada" first applied to present-day Ontario and Quebec?

25 The vessel *Grande Hermine* carried which explorer to Canada in 1535?

26 Who was the first European to reach Alberta?

27 What part of Canada did Jacques Cartier call "the land God gave to Cain"?
A. Cape Breton Island
B. The North Shore of the St. Lawrence
C. Labrador

28 Choose which of the following explorers was the first to confirm there was a Northwest Passage through Canadian Arctic waters, and identify who was the first to navigate that Passage.
A. Henry Larsen
B. Robert McClure
C. Vilhjalmur Steffansson
D. Roald Amundsen

29 Who was the first European to see bison?
A. Henry Kelsey
B. Alexander Henry
C. Pierre de La Vérendrye

The first European sees buffalo.

"Canada" appears on an early map.

34 When did the east coast of Canada first appear on a map?

32 Who was the first recorded European to set foot on what was to become British Columbia?

33 What explorer claimed the Arctic for Canada?

The European discoverer of British Columbia.

30 Who was the explorer of the Canadian north who died after his crew mutinied and set him adrift in a small boat, never to be seen again?
A. Vitus Bering
C. William Baffin
D. Martin Frobisher
E. Henry Hudson

Canada's north is explored.

31 In the eighteenth century, which fur trade explorer became the first European to reach Canada's Arctic coast overland?
A. Samuel Hearne
B. Alexander Mackenzie
C. David Thompson
E. Henry Kelsey

35 The first tourists to Canada were 30 London gentlemen who chartered a ship under the direction of Richard Hore in 1536 to "see the strange things of the world." What happened to them?

36 Where does the expression "as false as a diamond of Canada" come from?

37 When and where was the first European child born in Canada?

1 The shell necklaces called wampum were used by early First Nations for trade and exchange. They have been found as far inland as the Great Plains.

2 Port Royal, Nova Scotia, established by Pierre de Monts and Samuel de Champlain in 1605, was the first permanent European settlement in Canada.

NAC

Samuel de Champlain

3 After the capture of Quebec by General Wolfe in 1759 in the Seven Years War, a number of London importers lobbied the government to exchange Canada for the island of Guadeloupe in the West Indies. The French island produced rich sugar and coffee crops that were at the time as valuable as the furs from Canada's interior. However, Britain had other sources of coffee and sugar, and the British Navy needed a secure source of oak, so at the Peace of Paris in 1763, Britain kept Canada. France was allowed to keep only the tiny islands of St. Pierre and Miquelon and part of Louisiana.

4 "Kanata" is an Iroquois word meaning village or community. Jacques Cartier is believed to have named New France Canada in 1536 from this Iroquois word. When he came across the site of Montreal in the same year, Cartier was impressed with the fortified Iroquois village of Hochelaga because it closely resembled European culture. The fields round about were fertile and well tilled. It is believed that Cartier travelled to Canada with Verrazzano as early as 1524 and that he may have been in Newfoundland prior to 1534 when he first sailed up the St. Lawrence.

5 The last member of the Beothuks, a tribe that lived in Newfoundland and originally numbered 50,000, died in 1827. The entire population was wiped out by war and disease.

6 Mohawk leader Thayendanega was also called Joseph Brant. Born near present-day Akron, Ohio, he grew up in the Mohawk Valley of New York State. After the Revolution he and his Iroquois Loyalists settled on a tract of land on the Grand River, near the present city of Brantford.

7 Fort Detroit was captured by Tecumseh, a Shawnee leader and ally of the British and Canadian forces in the War of 1812. Tecumseh was later killed at the Battle of Moraviantown on the Thames.

8 Reports of the Cypress Hills Massacre in what is now southeastern Alberta, and the deaths of over 20 people, helped increase public support for the newly organized police force called the North West Mounted Police.

9 Possibly the Newfoundland Beothuk peoples were the first native North Americans to reach Europe. There is an 1153 AD medieval legend from Lubeck, Germany, telling the story of the arrival in Europe of a canoe with Indians from the coast of what we now call Newfoundland—a land on the same latitude as Germany. Other accounts suggest they were rescued from a canoe drifting in the Atlantic Ocean.

10 The ancient Chinese geographical text Shan Hai Ching T'sang-chu and the classic chronicle Shan Hai Jing both hold evidence that the two Chinese Imperial astronomers Hsi and Ho were the first known explorers of America in 2640 BC. Emperor Huang Ti ordered Hsi and Ho to make astronomical observations in the land of Fu Sang to the east of China. They sailed north to the Bering Strait, then south along the North American coastline. For a while they lived with Pueblo Indians close to the Grand Canyon, before returning to China. Their astronomical and geographic observations and discoveries were well received at the Imperial Palace, but the Emperor later executed them for failing to accurately predict a partial solar eclipse. Other records place the Asian contact only 1,500 years ago, with the journey of Hussein, an Afghan priest, and four Buddhist monks from Kabul to British Columbia in a junk in the year of Everlasting Origin, 459 AD.

11 The Sinclair Society claims that navigator Henry Sinclair's logs in Venice record his trip to Nova Scotia in 1398. Born at Rosslyn Castle near Edinburgh in 1345, Henry Sinclair became Earl of Rosslyn and the surrounding lands as well as Prince of Orkney, Duke of Oldenburg (Denmark) and Premier Earl of Norway. He lived among the Mi'kmaq of Nova Scotia long enough to be remembered in legend as the man-god Glooscap.

12 In two medieval Icelandic narratives, Norse merchant Bjarni Herjulfson sailed from Iceland toward Greenland on a visit to his father in 986 AD. He was blown off course in a storm and found himself along the coast of a hilly, forested land, possibly Nova Scotia. He turned back quickly, anxious to reach Greenland before winter. Seven years later, Leif Ericson acquired Bjarni Herjulfson's ship and sailed west with a 35-man crew, landing at a place he called Vinland. His brother Thorvald sailed the same ship to Vinland in the autumn of 1004 and wintered over there. While exploring the St. Lawrence River the following summer, they attacked a band of Native people and killed eight of them. The Beothuk retaliated some time later and Thorvald was killed. Two years later the survivors took Thorvald's body back to Greenland for burial.

13 Great Admiral Giovanni Caboto Montecataluna, or John Cabot, discovered Newfoundland. In 1497, King Henry VII

Commemorative stamp of the discovery of Newfoundland.

commissioned Cabot, an Italian, and his sons Sebastian and Sancio, to sail to all parts of the eastern, western and northern sea. They departed from Bristol, England, sailed 700 leagues west and arrived with a crew of 18 at Newfoundland. They navigated its coast for 300 leagues without seeing a single person but they did discover signs of inhabitants.

14 One 1502 map of Canada shows the lands southwest of Greenland and labels Canada as Terra Del Roy de Portugall, or, land belonging to the king of Portugal. In 1500 Alberto Cantino returned to Lisbon, Portugal, with 57 Beothuk slaves from Newfoundland for display. In 1501 Gaspar Corte-Real reached the coast of Labrador and became governor of Canada under permit of the Portuguese king. In 1506, Portugal began levying customs duties on codfish from North America. Newfoundland was called the Isle of Baccalaos, "baccalaos" meaning codfish in Portuguese.

15 In 1504, French Breton sailors built a fort called Brest on the north shore of the Strait of Belle Isle in Baie de Vieux Fort, Labrador, the first French settlement in Canada. However, Basque, Norman and Breton fishermen had used this harbour much earlier than 1500. In 1506, Jean Denys of Honfleur sailed to the New Lands, returning with codfish and geographical charts of his discovery.

16 François I sent Jacques Cartier on his expedition to discover a North American route to the Orient in 1534. Cartier made three trips to Canada and was the first French navigator to sail up the Gulf of St. Lawrence.

17 Convicted criminals were the colonists in Marquis de la Roche's failed attempt to settle Sable Island.

18 England's first colony in what is now Canada was established in 1610 at Cupers Cove, Conception Bay, Newfoundland. Now called Cupid's Cove, it was settled by John Guy and 39 colonists.

19 Pierre Gaultier de Varennes et de La Vérendrye (1685–1749). He and his sons Louis-Joseph and François got a three-year monopoly on the fur trade west of Superior in 1728 and built a chain of posts from Lake Superior to the lower Saskatchewan River as far as present-day Portage La Prairie.

20 Lake Winnipeg was first discovered by François de Varennes de La Vérendrye in about 1729. He and his brother Louis-Joseph were also credited with discovering the Rocky Mountains in 1743, but research shows they only glimpsed the snow-covered Big Horn Range in South Dakota.

21 Étienne Brûlé was the first European to explore the Great Lakes and visit the site of Toronto, descending "le passage de Toronto," a well-worn portage to Lake Ontario via the Holland River, with 12 Huron warriors, to meet allies and gather support. In old Iroquois, the word "toronto" means, roughly, "a good place to do business." It may also be a Huron word meaning "fish weir" or "place to trap smelt."

22 Alexander MacKenzie was the first explorer to cross Canada by land.

23 Saskatchewan.

24 The Constitutional Act of 1791 divided the former province of Quebec into two parts at the Ottawa River: Upper Canada and Lower Canada. Each province had a lieutenant-governor, assisted by an executive council, a legislative council and a house of assembly. Upper Canada's capital was to be at Newark (Niagara); Lower Canada's at Quebec City. In 1791, Upper Canada had a population of about 10,000 people, mostly United Empire Loyalists. The first lieutenant-governor of Upper Canada was John Graves Simcoe; of Lower Canada, Alured Clarke; and both were under Guy Carleton, Baron Dorchester, Governor-in-Chief of Canada. These two provinces were joined once again to form the Province of Canada in 1841 and were then referred to as Canada West (Upper Canada, or Ontario) and Canada East (Lower Canada, or Quebec).

25 Jacques Cartier's ship was called *La Grande Hermine*.

26 In 1754, Anthony Henday, an employee of the Hudson's Bay Company, sighted the Rocky Mountains at present-day Innisfail, Alberta, near Red Deer. He wintered with the Archithinue (Blackfoot) and then returned to York Fort on Hudson Bay.

27 The desolateness of the North Shore of the St. Lawrence provoked Jacques Cartier to call it "the land God gave to Cain."

28 McClure won the prize offered by the British Parliament for confirmation of the Passage; Amundsen was the first to navigate it, from 1903 to 1906, in the *Gjoa*.

29 Henry Kelsey was the first European to see bison, and rode with Native people on bison hunts.

30 Henry Hudson, after whom Hudson Bay is named, died after his crew mutinied and set him adrift.

31 Samuel Hearne was the first to reach Canada's Arctic coast by land. He is also credited as being the first European to discover Great Slave Lake.

32 After surveying the St. Lawrence River and Grand Banks of Newfoundland, Captain James Cook commanded three expeditions to the Pacific, mapping the New Zealand and Australian coastline. On his third voyage in 1778, he landed at Nootka Sound on the west coast of Vancouver Island. He had friendly relations with the local Nootka people but was killed by Hawaiian natives a few months later. A Spanish fleet, under the command of Juan Perez, had sailed along the coast of Vancouver Island in 1774, and likely went ashore for fresh water.

33 On July 1, 1909, at Melville Island, Nunavut, Joseph-Elzéar Bernier, captain of the government steamship Arctic, placed a metal plaque at Parry Rock claiming Canadian sovereignty over the entire *Arctic* archipelago. "I took possession of Baffin Island for Canada in the presence of several Eskimo," said Bernier, "and after firing 19 shots I instructed an Eskimo to fire the 20, telling him that he was now a Canadian." Bernier led several expeditions into the Arctic between 1904 and 1911, to certify Canada's claim to the northern archipelago. At the time, US and Norwegian whalers and mining companies were trying to convince their governments to claim the land.

34 In 1507 Bernadinus Venetus Vitalibus of Rome printed the Ruysch world map, which clearly displays the East Coast of North America including Hudson Bay. Newfoundland is recorded as Terra Nova and Greenland is attached to the mainland. Many inland rivers are recorded and named. This map was a composite of all known exploration records residing in Rome.

35 The party ran out of provisions in Newfoundland and the healthier men had to resort to cannibalism. A well-provisioned French fishing ship saved Hore and the surviving tourists. They callously took over the ship, left its crew to fend for themselves on the shore and sailed home.

36 In 1542 Newfoundland sailors reported that Jacques Cartier and the Sieur de Roberval had accumulated 11 barrels of gold ore and a quantity of precious stones, rubies and diamonds. Back in France, the gold and stones turned out to be pyrites and quartz, which gave rise to the saying "as false as a diamond of Canada." A year earlier Jacques Cartier had established Fort Charlesbourg Royal (Cap Rouge) nine miles above Quebec City, and the minerals were found in nearby rocks.

37 According to Norse saga, Leif Ericson's brother-in-law Thorfinn Karlsefni set off for Vinland in 1010 with 60 men and 5 women. They reached Vinland safely—at present-day L'Anse-aux-Meadows, Newfoundland, where Thorfinn's wife gave birth to a son whom they named Snorri—the first known European child to be born in the Americas. The expedition returned to Greenland four years later after attacks from the local Native people. Over 500 hundred years later, Marguerite de La Rocque, a relative of the Sieur de Roberval, accompanied him on his voyage to Canada in 1542. Shocked by Marguerite taking a lover, Roberval set her ashore on Ile des Demons in the St. Lawrence River, with her lover and a servant girl. The lover, the servant girl and Marguerite's child born on the island died. Marguerite was rescued and was taken back to France by fishermen. This may be the first recorded birth of a European child in New France.

1 On August 29, 1583, in one of Canada's first marine disasters, an English ship, *The Delight*, was lost at Sable Island, drowning 85 people. Who did the ship belong to?

2 St. John's, Newfoundland, was devastated by major fires in 1817, 1846 and 1892. What other disastrous fire left 15,000 people homeless in New Brunswick in 1825?

A maritime disaster in the Atlantic in 1873.

Maritime Museum of the Atlantic, Halifax

3 Where was Canada's worst railway disaster?

4 What maritime disaster off Halifax in 1873 killed over 500 people?

5 What Nova Scotia town has suffered two major mining disasters?

6 A landslide in 1903 killed over 70 citizens of this Alberta town.

NAC

Site of two of Canada's worst mining disasters.

1903

A view of the 1903 devastating Alberta landslide.

7 What was Canada's worst bridge disaster?

Canada's worst bridge disaster.

10 Canada's worst maritime disaster occurred on May 29, 1914, when at least 950 perished as a ship went down off Rimouski in the St. Lawrence River. In 1997, a Quebec entrepreneur developed a

11 What was Canada's single worst mining disaster?

12 What historic building burned down on February 3, 1916?

The ocean liner that perished in Canada's worst maritime disaster.

controversial plan to salvage nickel ingots from the wreckage of this historic St. Lawrence shipwreck. Name the ship.

8 Over 200 victims of the sinking of what ship are buried in Halifax, Nova Scotia, cemeteries?

9 On June 30, 1912, a killer tornado ripped through the downtown core of Regina in a five-minute rampage, killing 28, injuring 200 and damaging or destroying three churches, the new Carnegie Library, commercial buildings and homes. Twenty-five hundred were left homeless and Mayor Peter McAra cancelled Dominion Day celebrations. When was the next major tornado disaster to hit a major Canadian city?

13 What was the site of the world's largest man-made explosion until the Americans dropped the bomb on Hiroshima in 1945?

Aftermath of the greatest explosion until Hiroshima.

15 When and where was Canada's deadliest recorded earthquake?

16 Name the hurricane that devastated Toronto in 1954.
A. Henry
B. Hilda
C. Hugo
D. Hazel

17 When and where was Canada's worst air disaster?

18 Canada's worst Great Lakes disaster came on September 14, 1949, when the *Noronic*, the largest Canadian passenger ship on the Great Lakes, was consumed by fire while docked in Toronto harbour, killing 118. What later marine disaster is remembered in a haunting 1976 ballad by Gordon Lightfoot?

19 A quarter of a million people were forced to evacuate what Canadian city because of a rail accident in 1979?

20 On February 15, 1982, 84 men working on this sea platform were killed in the worst marine disaster in Canada since World War II. What was it called?

14 What event in 1918 killed over 30,000 people in Canada?

TO MAKE A MASK

ISSUED BY THE PROVINCIAL BOARD OF HEALTH

24 What natural disaster hit the Saguenay region of Quebec in 1996?

25 The worst road accident in Canadian history claimed 43 lives on Thanksgiving weekend, 1997, outside St-Bernard-de-Beauce, just south of Quebec City. What happened?

26 On May 2, 1997, a special CBC Radio *Morningside* concert raised over $450,000 for victims of one of the costliest natural disasters in Canadian history. What was the disaster?

27 What natural disaster in Ontario and Quebec in 1998 killed 25 people and did an estimated $2 billion in damage?

21 What airline crash off the coast of Ireland in 1985 killed 329, including 280 Canadians?

22 Name the killer of 14 women on December 6, 1989, at L'École Polytechnique at the University of Montreal.

23 On May 9, 1992, a devastating explosion, caused by a buildup of methane gas, ripped through the southwest section of a coal mine in Plymouth, Nova Scotia, killing 26 miners underground. Name the mine.

1 *The Delight*, lost at Sable Island in August 1583, was owned by Sir Humphrey Gilbert. Earlier that same month Gilbert had formally taken possession of Newfoundland, the first English possession in the New World. Since 1583 there have been over 350 recorded shipwrecks on Sable Island, Nova Scotia, earning it the title "Graveyard of the Atlantic."

2 The Great Miramichi Fire began on September 19, 1825. One-fifth of New Brunswick, or about 6,000 square miles, burned—from north of Miramichi to the outskirts of Fredericton—and the towns of Fredericton, Newcastle, Douglastown, Moorfield, Bartibog, Nappan, Black River, Oromocto River and surrounding areas were almost totally destroyed.

3 On June 29, 1864, at Beloeil, Quebec, a Grand Trunk Railway train ran through an open switch near St-Hilaire, killing 99 people. It was Canada's worst railway disaster.

4 On April 1, 1873, the luxury liner *Atlantic*, sailing from Liverpool to New York, turned into Halifax Harbour to get coal, but struck a reef near Mars Rock, Meagher's Island. Five hundred and forty-six people were drowned in heavy seas, while local fishermen manage to save 300.

5 Springhill, Nova Scotia, has witnessed two of Canada's worst mining disasters. On February 21, 1891, a coal gas explosion killed 129 miners. On October 23, 1958, 174 miners were trapped by a coal gas explosion and rock surge in the Number Two Cumberland mine—the deepest coal mine in North America. Rescue workers brought 81 men out the first day, 12 more were found alive on October 30, 7 more on November 1. But 74 men died underground.

6 On April 29, 1903, at 4:10 a.m., a huge 74-million-ton slab of limestone slid off the east slope of Turtle Mountain and swept 1.6 kilometres through the Crowsnest Pass valley and the coal mining village of Frank, burying the mine entrance and killing at least 70 people in 100 seconds; only 23 survived, but 17 trapped miners dug themselves to safety 13 hours later. The slab was 400 metres high, 1,200 metres wide and 150 metres thick.

7 On August 29, 1907, the south cantilever arm of the Quebec Bridge over the St. Lawrence River collapsed during construction; over 65 workers were killed and 11 injured. The bridge was rebuilt in 1916 but the centre span fell into the river, killing another 13 people. When it was finally completed in September 1917, the Quebec Bridge was the world's longest cantilever bridge, and the largest bridge in the world.

8 On May 3, 1912, the first *Titanic* victims were buried in Halifax. The White Star Line had chartered four ships from Halifax to recover the remains of the *Titanic* victims. The ships recovered 328 bodies; bodies too badly damaged or deteriorated were buried at sea, and 209 were brought to Halifax. A temporary morgue was set up in the Mayflower Curling Rink, and identified bodies shipped out to families or interred in Halifax; burials continued to June 12, 1912. Nineteen victims were laid to rest in the Mount Olivet Catholic Cemetery, 10 in the Baron de Hirsch Jewish Cemetery, and 121 in the Fairview Lawn Cemetery; 42 remain unidentified.

9 A mammoth tornado struck Edmonton on July 31, 1987, during the afternoon rush hour, killing 27 people, injuring at least 250 and causing $150 million worth of damage; most casualties lived in an Edmonton East trailer park.

10 The Canadian Pacific ocean liner, *Empress of Ireland*, sank on May 29, 1914, after being hit by the Norwegian coal ship *Storstad* in the Gulf of St. Lawrence. The *Empress of Ireland* sank 11 minutes later after the *Storstad* backed out of the hole in the hull. One thousand and twenty-four lives were lost, 464 saved; $1 million in silver bars was later recovered by divers. This was Canada's worst, and—after the *Titanic* and *Lusitania*—the Atlantic's third largest maritime disaster.

11 At least 190 men died in a coal dust explosion on June 19, 1914, at the Hillcrest Coal Mine in Alberta.

12 The Centre Block of the Parliament Buildings burned down in 1916.

13 The Halifax Explosion on December 6, 1917, was the world's largest man-made explosion until Hiroshima. World War I was still raging  in Europe, and the harbourfront of Halifax was bustling with supply ships loading troops, relief supplies and munitions. At 8:45 a.m., a French munitions freighter, the *Mont Blanc*, carrying 2,300 tons of picric acid, 200 tons of TNT, 35 tons of high octane gasoline, and 10 tons of gun cotton, collided with the Belgium relief ship *Imo*. The *Mont Blanc* was propelled toward the shore by the collision and the crew abandoned the blazing ship, failing to alert the harbour of the peril. Minutes later the blazing ship brushed by a pier, setting it ablaze, while spectators gathered along the waterfront to witness the spectacle. The Halifax Fire Department crew were just positioning their engine up to the nearest hydrant when the *Mont Blanc* exploded at 9:05 a.m. in a blinding white flash. The blast levelled downtown Halifax, killing 2,000, injuring over 8,000, leaving 10,000 homeless, and causing $50 million worth of damage. The shock wave shattered windows at Truro, 100 kilometres away, and was heard as far away as Charlottetown.

14 The global Spanish Flu epidemic first hit Canadian soldiers in Europe in July, and on September 1, about 400 teachers and students in Victoriaville, Quebec, came down with the disease, brought to Canada by returning troops. On October 7, influenza claimed its first victim in Montreal. Across Canada, churches, schools and theatres closed. On October 31, the Alberta government prohibited all public meetings of seven persons or more. The flu raged until about 1925 and probably claimed over 50,000 victims.

15 An 1929 undersea quake off Newfoundland's Burin Peninsula caused tidal waves that killed 29 people.

16 On October 15, Hurricane Hazel raged across the Appalachians and hit south-central Ontario. Packing winds of 124 kilometres an hour, the storm dropped 10.1 centimetres of rain in 12 hours, the heaviest rains in southern Ontario history. On Raymore Drive in Etobicoke, 17 homes were swept into the Humber River, and 36 were killed when debris blocked a bridge and more homes washed away. The storm did $25 million worth of damage and killed 83 people.

17 On November 29, 1963, at St-Thérèse, north of Montreal, a Trans-Canada Airlines DC-8F with 111 passengers and seven crew crashed in the bush four minutes after takeoff from Dorval Airport; there were no survivors, and no satisfactory explanation of the disaster.

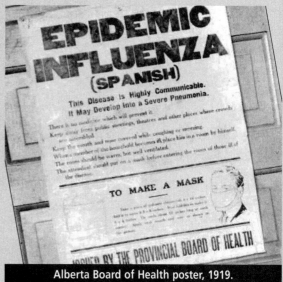

Alberta Board of Health poster, 1919.

18 On November 10, 1975, in Lake Superior off Whitefish Point, Ontario, west of Sault Ste. Marie, the Great Lakes ship *Edmund Fitzgerald*, a 222-metre-long iron ore carrier out of Superior, Wisconsin, broke in two and sank after battling 7.5-metre waves and record 125-kilometre-an-hour winds during a November gale; 29 crew members drowned.

19 On November 10, 1979, Canadian Pacific freight number 54 derailed en route from Windsor to Agincourt. Nineteen of the 24 CP Rail tanker cars contained dangerous propane, soda and chlorine, and after an explosion and fire the following day, they started leaking chlorine gas. Mississauga's mayor ordered an official evacuation of the city; 240,000 residents had to leave, some for six days. No one was killed or injured in the largest single movement of people in Canadian history.

20 The Ocean Ranger oil rig capsized and sank in 18-metre waves during a fierce storm on the Grand Banks 315 kilometres east of St. John's on February 15, 1982. All the crew, 56

of whom were Newfoundlanders, drowned in the worst marine disaster in Canada since World War II. The rig was owned by New Orleans–based Ocean Drilling and Exploration Company (ODECO) and under contract to Mobil Oil Canada to drill the Hibernia oil field; enquiry later found seawater entered the ballast control room through a broken porthole and shorted the panel controlling the rig's stability.

21 The June 23 crash of an Air-India jet in 1985 en route to Bombay from Toronto killed 329, including 280 Canadians. Sikh extremists were accused of planting a bomb on board the plane.

22 In a classroom at L'École Polytechnique on December 6, 1989, Marc Lepine separated the men from the women, whom he called feminists, then opened fire, killing 14, before turning the gun on himself. Twelve others were left injured.

23 The Westray Mine explosion occurred on May 9, 1992. The bodies of 11 men were recovered immediately; an unsuccessful search for survivors continued for six days. In October, four Westray officials were charged with violating mine safety rules by failing to clear explosive dust.

24 From July 19 to July 21, 1996, 277 millimetres of rain fell in a 72-hour period over the Charlevoix and Lower North Shore regions of Saguenay, Quebec, causing dam bursts and devastating floods that killed 10, left about 10,000 homeless and did $500 million in damage.

25 A bus carrying seniors crashed off the road into a ravine just south of Quebec City in 1997. Only five people survived.

26 The Red River flood in Manitoba; performers included Murray McLauchlan, singing his ballad "Red River Valley," and Valdy, who composed a new song, "As the Waters Fall," for the occasion. The flooding of this river caused thousands to evacuate their homes in 1950 and 1979.

27 A severe winter ice storm in 1998 left three million people in Ontario and Quebec without electrical power for days and in some cases weeks on end, after transmission towers and power lines buckled under the weight of the ice.

1 Which French military leader defeated the English in a naval battle in Hudson Bay in 1697?

2 Who said, "I have no reply to make other than from the mouths of my cannons!"?
A. Sir Isaac Brock
B. Count Frontenac
C. General Wolfe
D. General Montcalm

3 The French Fortress of Louisbourg was captured by the British for the last time in 1758. In which province is it located?

4 On September 13, 1759, which two generals fought on the Plains of Abraham?

5 When did The Seven Years War occur?

The battle at Queenston Heights, 1812.

6 An American force led by two generals failed in its attempt to capture Quebec. They attacked on January 1, 1776. One general was Richard Montgomery; who was the other?

7 What hero of the War of 1812 walked over 30 kilometres through enemy territory lines to warn English commander James FitzGibbon of an impending ambush by American forces?

8 Niagara-on-the-Lake and the town of York, now Toronto, were both sacked and burned by American soldiers in the War of 1812. What did the British do to avenge the capture and burning of the town of York?

British forces on the Plains of Abraham.

French troops on the Plains of Abraham.

9 Name the British general killed in battle at Queenston Heights in 1812.

10 The treaty signed on which date marked the end of the War of 1812?
A. December 24, 1814
B. October 25, 1813
C. June 23, 1813
D. April 12, 1813

11 Why was the Rideau Canal built?

12 On which side did most Canadians fight during the American Civil War?

13 The highest award given to any serving officer or member of the British or Commonwealth Armed Forces is the Victoria Cross, given for valour in the face of the enemy. It was instituted in 1856 by Queen Victoria. Who was the first Canadian to win the Victoria Cross?

14 These Irish-Americans attacked Fort Erie, Ontario, in 1866.

15 In 1884, 400 Canadian volunteers accompanied a British Army expedition up which river?
A. Congo
B. Ganges
C. Nile
D. Pearl

16 Who was the Métis leader who commanded Louis Riel's troops in the

The Battle of Batoche, 1885.

1885 Northwest Rebellion?

17 What was the first overseas war in which Canadians were involved?

18 On April 21, 1918, German air ace Manfred von Richthofen, the Red Baron, was shot down either by Canadian squadron leader Captain Roy Brown, or by Australian ground fire. Who was the famous young Canadian aviator the Red Baron was chasing when he was shot down?

Canada's first and famous World War I victory, Easter 1917.

19 What military victory on Easter Monday, April 9, 1917, led to a great outpouring of Canadian nationalism?

20 Which World War I battle inspired Guelph, Ontario, physician John McCrae to write his poem "In Flanders Fields"?

Canadian World War I flying ace.

21 What old city did Canadian troops capture on the last day of World War I?
A. Cambrai
B. Ypres
C. Lens
D. Mons

22 Considered "Canada's own," this firearm was withdrawn from World War I service because of poor battlefield performance.

23 In 1914, the Canadian Naval Service began to use CC1s and CC2s. What were they?

24 Who was Canada's top air ace in World War I?

25 Approximately how many Canadian servicemen were killed in World War I?
A. 24,000
B. 60,000
C. 92,000

26 Who were the Zombies in World War I?
A. An elite force of guerillas
B. V-1 buzz bombs
C. Home defence conscripts

27 Who is Canada's most decorated war hero?

28 The Books of Remembrance honouring Canada's war dead are located in this Tower.

29 Who formed the Mackenzie-Papineau Battalion and where did they fight?

30 How long after Britain did Canada declare war in 1939?
A. One day later
B. One week later
C. Two weeks later
D. Two months later

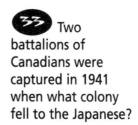

Royal Canadian Air Force No. 1 Fighter Squadron. (NAC)

31 The Royal Canadian Air Force came into being on April 1, 1924. The RCAF No. 1 Fighter Squadron reached England in June 1940, in time to participate in what battle?

32 Who was "the man called Intrepid," a.k.a. The Quiet Canadian, and what secret camp did he build in Ontario?

33 Two battalions of Canadians were captured in 1941 when what colony fell to the Japanese?

34 Starting in 1942, the Canadian government relocated 20,881 people to detention camps in the BC interior, Alberta and Manitoba. What nationality were these people?

35 Canada's greatest military disaster occurred during a raid involving 5,000 Canadian troops intended to test the German defences on the coast of Europe. Where and when did it occur?

36 Which World War II Allied action involving Canadians was code-named Operation Husky?
A. Invasion of Sicily
B. North Africa coast landings
C. Liberation of Holland and Belgium
D. Crossing the Rhine

37 On June 6, 1944, Canadian troops were part of the Allied forces that attacked the Normandy coast of France on D-Day. What was the code name for this military manoeuvre and for the beach where the Canadians landed?

Canadian troops on D-Day landing.

NAC

43 During the October Crisis beginning on October 5, 1970, the Federal government invoked an Act of Parliament that suspended civil liberties and rights. What is the name of that Act?

44 The Snowbirds—Canada's 431 Air Demonstration Squadron—is a nine-plane military aerobatic team out of CFB Moose Jaw, Saskatchewan, that performs at air shows all over Canada and the USA every year. When did they receive their name?

38 This country was liberated by Canadian forces in 1945.

39 Franklin Roosevelt, Winston Churchill and Mackenzie King met twice at what Quebec City hotel during World War II?

42 Canadians have been part of a peacekeeping force on the island of Cyprus since 1964, keeping peace between Greek and Turkish factions. Earlier Canadian troops and aircraft were sent to the Congo as part of a UN peacekeeping operation from 1960 to 1964. Where and when did General E.L.M. Burns lead Canada's first peacekeeping force?

40 What was the 5BX?

41 In 1957, the DEW Line went into operation to alert North American air defences against Soviet bomber attacks coming over the Pole. What does DEW stand for?

Armed soldiers at the National Arts Centre in Ottawa, October 1970.

NAC

1 Pierre le Moyne d'Iberville in his ship *The Pelican* defeated three British ships and captured York Fort, near Churchill on Hudson Bay in 1696.

2 Count Frontenac, in scornful reply to demands for the surrender of Quebec, said, "I have no reply to make other than from the mouths of my cannons!"

3 The French Fortress of Louisbourg is in the province of Nova Scotia, on Cape Breton Island south of Sydney.

4 The forces of the Marquis de Montcalm and General James Wolfe faced each other on the Plains of Abraham. On the morning of September 13, 1759, James Wolfe landed at l'Anse au Foulon, a cove three kilometres west of Quebec, having kept his battle plans secret from even his trusted English lieutenants. His men quickly climbed an overgrown path up the cliff face and surprised a company of the opposing French militia. While British frigates started firing on Quebec city, in a cold drizzle, Wolfe reached the top of the cliff with the last of his 4,500 troops; before him stretched the Plains of Abraham. When Montcalm was told that the English were on the Plains of Abraham, he ordered troops to form up outside the walls. As the French started to advance, Wolfe was hit by a shell fragment in the abdomen. The French held their fire until they were within 25 metres of the British lines. At 12 metres, Wolfe gave the order to fire, and one great volley ripped through the French ranks. The last volleys were fired with the two armies only feet apart, then Wolfe gave the order to charge with bayonet, and the French turned to flee. Wolfe was leading the grenadiers when a bullet hit him in the chest and he fell. Someone yelled, "See how they run." Wolfe opened his eyes and asked, "Who runs?"; a soldier replied, "The French run, sir." It is said that Wolfe replied, "Now God be praised, I die in peace," and closed his eyes forever. Wolfe died within minutes and his body was shipped back to England, pickled in a whiskey barrel. Montcalm was wounded outside the walls. He asked two soldiers to hold him up in the saddle as he went in the St. Louis Gate, so as not to cause more panic. When the surgeon told him he had only a few hours to live, Montcalm replied, "So much the better, I shall not see the surrender of Quebec." He died early the next morning. "Measured by the numbers engaged, the Battle of Quebec was but a heavy skirmish," wrote historian Francis Parkman, "measured by results, it was one of the great battles of the world."

5 The Seven Years War (King George's War) lasted from 1756 to 1763. Britain and France declared war on one another on May 17, 1756. What is called the French and Indian War by Americans is also known to the British as King George's War and was part of a still bigger European conflict known as the Seven Years War, a struggle for world economic and colonial power between France and Britain. The surrender of Montreal in 1760 ended the French-Indian War, while the Seven Years War continued in other parts of the world until February 10, 1763.

6 Benedict Arnold, the famous American traitor, was one of two American generals who attacked Quebec. After turning traitor he fled to Saint John, New Brunswick, during the American Revolution and returned to England five years later.

7 In 1813, the famous hero of the War of 1812 Laura Secord sneaked through enemy lines to warn the English of an American ambush.

8 To avenge the capture of York, British troops bombarded Baltimore and put Washington to the torch. On the evening of August 24, 1814, 5,000 British troops under the command of General Robert Ross marched into Washington, DC, after defeating an American force in Maryland. Meeting no resistance, the British burned the White House, the Capitol and almost every public building in the city before a downpour doused the flames. "The Star-Spangled Banner" was written by Francis Scott Key during the bombardment of Baltimore earlier in the year.

9 Sir Isaac Brock died at the battle at Queenston Heights in 1812. He is supposed to have uttered the words "Push on, brave York volunteers!" as he lay dying.

10 The Treaty of Ghent marked the end of the War of 1812 and was signed December 24, 1814.

11 The Rideau Canal was built, following the War of 1812, to provide a safe route to get supplies to the military in Upper Canada, bypassing the series of rapids and the American shoreline on parts of the St. Lawrence River.

12 During the American Civil War 50,000 Canadians fought for the North. Fewer than 1,000 Canadians fought for the South.

13 On January 29, 1856, Queen Victoria awarded Britain's highest military honour to Alexander Dunn (1833–1868) for gallantry in the charge of the Light Brigade in the Crimea in 1854. He was the first Canadian to receive this honour.

14 The Fenians, who wanted to overthrow British rule in Ireland, attacked Fort Erie, Ontario, in 1866.

15 Canadian voyageurs accompanied a British Army expedition up the Nile River in 1884.

16 Gabriel Dumont was the commander of Riel's troops in the Northwest Rebellion. The Battle of Batoche started on May 9, 1885, when General Frederick Dobson Middleton attacked Dumont at Batoche. The battle raged for several days, until Middleton's troops disobeyed him, stormed the trenches and slaughtered the Métis defenders. Riel later gave himself up and was charged with treason; he was executed at Regina on November 16.

17 The 1898 Boer War was the first overseas war to involve Canadian soldiers. They distinguished themselves at the battle of Paardeberg in South Africa.

18 Wilfrid Reid "Wop" May flew in the World War I battle in which the Red Baron was shot down. Later a pioneer bush pilot, May won the McKee Trophy in 1929 for delivering diphtheria antitoxin to Fort Vermillion, Alberta, in the dead of winter. In World War II, May helped set up the Commonwealth Air Training Plan.

19 The capture of Vimy Ridge by Arthur Currie's 100,000 strong Canadian Army galvanized Canadian military patriotism in World War I. Currie led all four divisions of the Canadian Corps, who were fighting as a unit for the first time, with one British brigade under Lieutenant-General Julian Byng. They captured Vimy Ridge on Easter Monday on April 9, 1917. Using 1,000 guns and a masterful artillery barrage technique developed by Currie and his gunners, they took the German stronghold where both the French and British had earlier failed. Four thousand Canadians were killed and 6,000 wounded in the attack. From that day onward, Germany was on the defensive.

20 "In Flanders Fields" was written after the bloody Second Battle of Ypres. There were three battles for the town of Ypres in Belgium in 1915. In the first Battle of Ypres Canadian troops had their first experience of a gas attack. The Third Battle of Ypres is better known as the Battle of Passchendaele.

21 On the last day of World War I Canadian troops captured Mons, the same city where the war began.

22 The Ross Rifle was manufactured in Canada and standard issue for Canadian soldiers in World War I until it was withdrawn from service because of poor performance.

23 The CC1 and CC2 were submarines in the Canadian navy in World War I.

24 Air Vice-Marshal William Avery "Billy" Bishop VC, DSO, shot down 72 German aircraft during World War I, 25 in one 10-day period in 1918. In August 1918 he joined the British Air Ministry and helped form the Canadian Flying Corps as a separate brigade. Bishop flew the single-seat Nieuport Scout, a tiny biplane powered by a rotary engine and armed with a single Lewis machine gun mounted above the top wing. Highly manoeuvrable, the Nieuport was a superb combat plane for the period.

25 At the end of World War I, 60,000 Canadian servicemen had died in the conflict. In World War II, approximately 42,000 Canadian servicemen gave their lives.

26 Conscripts for the Canadian home defence service in World War I were called the Zombies.

27 Lieutenant Colonel William Barker won 12 decorations for gallantry before the enemy in World War I. He is Canada's most decorated war hero.

28 The Peace Tower in Ottawa holds the Books of Remembrance honouring Canada's war dead.

29 The Mackenzie-Papineau Battalion was made up of Canadian volunteers in the 1936–39 Spanish Civil War, a prelude to World War II.

30 Canada declared war on Germany one week after Britain in 1939.

31 The RCAF No. 1 Fighter Squadron joined in the Battle of Britain in June 1940.

32 Canadian Sir William Stephenson, "the man called Intrepid," was Britain's head of espionage in the US during World War II, and the personal link between Churchill and Roosevelt. Camp X, a secret spy training facility, was set up by Stephenson near Whitby, Ontario. Its most famous student was Ian Fleming, the man who created fictional British superspy James Bond.

33 Two Canadian battalions were captured in 1941 when Hong Kong fell to the Japanese.

34 Japanese-Canadians. In January 1941, Federal Minister Ian Mackenzie announced that the RCMP would be registering all Japanese-Canadians in British Columbia as a national security matter under the War Measures Act. In February 1942, the government proclaimed western British Columbia a "protected area" under wartime regulations and ordered Japanese nationals moved inland for security reasons; within weeks, the government included second and third generation Canadians of Japanese origin under the edict. They were treated as aliens and deprived of their property, including homes and fishing boats and cars, which in many cases were sold at auction.

35 On August 19, 1942, 900 Canadians were killed and 1,000 wounded raiding the French port of Dieppe on the coast of Normandy. The raid failed to achieve any of its objectives and was Canada's greatest military disaster.

36 The 1st Canadian Infantry Division participated in the invasion and capture of Sicily in July 1943, code-named Operation Husky.

37 On D-Day, June 6, 1944, about 14,000 Canadian troops landed on Juno Beach and Gold Beach as part of Operation Overlord's 100-mile front. The first Canadian soldiers joined in the landing on Juno Beach between Courseulles and St-Aubin-sur-Mer. RCN minesweepers helped clear the lanes in, and RCAF bombers and fighters softened up the German defences. The main task of the Canadian Army was to push through the gap between Bayeux and Caen. The 1st Canadian Parachute Battalion red berets were part of the advance landing during the night, capturing a bridge near Caen with the British. At about 7:40 a.m., the 3rd Canadian Infantry Division and 2nd and 3rd Armoured, under Major-General R.F.L. Keller, started landing in rough seas. The 8th Brigade captured Bernières-sur-Mer by 9:30 a.m., but mines and German anti-tank guns held up the advance inland, creating a traffic jam in the village streets; they took Bény by evening. The 7th Brigade captured Courseulles, Ste-Croix and Banville, with heavy losses. The 9th Brigade

made it through Bény to Villons-les-Buissons, less than four miles from Caen, and nearly at their goal—Carpiquet airport. Canadian casualties that day were less than expected— 715 wounded, 359 dead.

38 Canada liberated the Netherlands from German occupation in 1945.

39 The Chateau Frontenac was the site of two military conferences between Franklin Roosevelt, Winston Churchill and Mackenzie King during World War II.

40 The Royal Canadian Air Force's exercise manual was called the 5BX, for five basic exercises. It became a best-seller.

41 The DEW Line is an acronym for Distant Early Warning Line.

42 Canada's first peacekeeping force was sent to Egypt in 1957. Canadian soldiers also served in the Gaza Strip after the Israeli-Egyptian crisis of 1956 until the peacekeeping force there was disbanded in 1967.

43 The War Measures Act was invoked by Pierre Trudeau during the 1970 October Crisis. This legislation was first brought in at the outbreak of World War I.

44 Canada's aerobatic squadron was named the Snowbirds as a result of a contest held at the CFB Moose Jaw Elementary School in 1971. At the time Anne Murray had a hit song by the same name. The Canadian Forces Parachute Team, which has performed over 3,000 demonstrations across Canada and throughout the US and Europe, is named The Sky Hawks.

CANADA INVENTS

1 The first Canadian patent was granted in 1791. Who was it awarded to, and for what invention?

2 Charles Fenerty got his idea for mechanizing pulp and paper manufacturing, setting in motion this large Canadian industry, by watching what insects at work?

3 Nova Scotian Abraham Gesner invented and developed kerosene oil for lighting in 1846. His invention led to the collapse of what nineteenth-century industry?

4 David A. Fife, a farmer on the fourth concession of Otonabee Township near Peterborough, Ontario, wrote a friend in Glasgow, Scotland, asking him to send some spring wheat. His friend sent him a sample of a new kind of wheat from Poland, and Fife planted the few grains in the spring of 1842. All but five heads rusted badly, but those that remained matured 10 days earlier than the other wheat on the farm. What was significant about Fife's wheat?

5 In what year did a Canadian invent the odometer?

6 Maritimers thank Saint John native Robert Foulis (1796–1866) for inventing the first practical version of this life-saving noisemaker.

7 What Canadian invented the green ink that has been used since 1862 to print US banknotes?

8 Who invented the first practical ice skate?

9 What African-Canadian inventor's name came to be synonymous with genuine quality, or the real thing?

10 Name the Canadian who invented the light bulb.

11 Where did Alexander Graham Bell build the first telephone?

Alexander Graham Bell, New York, 1892.

The inventor of Standard Time.

Confederation Life

18 When did Toronto inventor Norman Breakley invent the paint roller?

19 Who invented the hydrofoil boat in 1908?

12 Who invented the world system of time zones and Standard Time?

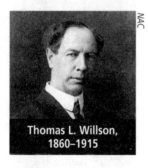

Thomas L. Willson, 1860–1915

NAC

An early hydrofoil test run.

Library of Congress

13 Thomas L. "Carbide" Willson, born in Woodstock, Ontario, in 1861, invented both carbide—used to make tough, long-lasting carbide-tipped blades—and the acetylene torch. What was he trying to invent that led to these two discoveries?

15 Did a Canadian invent Canada Dry Ginger Ale, and what was it originally called?

16 The Robertson screwdriver is named after which Canadian inventor?

Dr. Frederick Banting

Univ. of Penn.

21 What did Dr. Frederick Banting do with the patent rights for the manufacture of his invention insulin, first made available for diabetes treatment in late 1922?

14 In 1889, Nova Scotian Frederick Creed invented the precursor to all modern data communications. What was his invention called?

17 The Plexiglas in your shatterproof glasses was invented by William Chalmers at what Canadian university?

20 The gas mask was invented by Canadian Army physician Dr. Cluny McPherson after what battle in World War I?

Musée J-Armand Bombardier

An early Bombardier snow car.

22 In 1922, 15-year-old Valcourt, Quebec, mechanic Joseph-Armand Bombardier and his brother salvaged the motor from an old Ford, attached it to a propeller, bolted it over four runners from a sleigh, and took the first motorized zip through the town. What family tragedy led Bombardier to go on to invent the modern-day snowmobile?

23 Manitoba native Sir William Stephenson became known as "Intrepid" in the world of foreign espionage. He was also the inventor of what important newspaper and communications technology in 1923?

24 This invention of Arthur Sicard was first seen on the streets of Montreal, in the winter of 1925.

25 Who patented the world's first electric organ in 1928?

26 The name for the baby food Pablum comes from the Latin *pabulum*, or "substance that gives nourishment." Where in Canada was it invented?

PABLUM
Canada

27 Name the Canadian who obtained the first patent for the modern television camera in 1934.

28 Professor Eli Franklin Burton, heading a University of Toronto team of physicists, invented the electron microscope in what year?

29 What Canadian invented the space suit?

30 Name the Canadian who invented the electronic music synthesizer in 1945.

31 Who invented the green garbage bag in 1950?

32 Who invented the pacemaker for ailing hearts?

33 In 1961 Dr. Edward Asselbergs was trying to produce instant meat, fish or cheese. What instant food did he and his team discover by accident?

34 Two retired National Research Council of Canada scientists won an Academy Award in 1977 for their pioneering work in what area of film-making?

35 Where in Canada was the Trivial Pursuit board game invented?

36 Which computer programming language was invented by a Canadian in 1994?
A. Ada
B. Cobol
C. Java
D. Fortran

37 Canada's one-millionth patent was issued for biodegradable plastic in what year?

38 Who is Canada's greatest inventor?

39 Thomas Edison invented the electric light in 1879. Name Edison's chief chemist, the man who reinvented the electric light to create the modern light bulb.

40 On December 23, 1900, from a site on Cobb Island in the middle of the Potomac River near Washington, Reginald Fessenden made the first practical wireless broadcast, asking his assistant, one mile away, a typical Canadian question: "Is it snowing where you are, Mr. Thiessen? If it is, would you telegraph back to me?" This was almost a year before Marconi's transmission in Morse code from England to Signal Hill in Newfoundland, on December 12, 1901. If Fessenden invented radio, just what did Marconi invent?

NAC

41 In 1928, RCA's David Sarnoff kept Reginald Fessenden in court for 15 years before agreeing to pay him $500,000 for patents that allowed RCA to proceed with the development of what invention?

Radio inventor Reginald Fessenden, 1866–1932.

Ottawa Researchers

42 Name the Canadian inventor of the following:
- the radio pager
- sonar (stands for "sound navigation and ranging")
- the electrolytic detector
- the fathometer
- the seismograph
- the turbo-electric drive
- the gyrocompass
- the loop antenna
- radio direction-finding
- the pheroscope for submarines
- the TV receiver
- ultrasonic cleaning
- the electrical conduit
- carbon tetrachloride
- tracer bullets

1 The first Canadian patent was granted in 1791 by the Governor General in Council to Angus MacDonnel, a Scottish soldier garrisoned at Quebec City, and to Samuel Hopkins, a Vermonter, for processes to make potash fertilizer and soap from wood ash. Potash made from wood ash was a major cash crop for early Canadian pioneers.

2 In 1838 Charles Fenerty (1821–1892) mechanized a process he first observed being applied by wasps, who built paper-like nests by chewing up wood, thus launching Canada's pulp and paper industry.

3 Abraham Gesner was the first to refine kerosene oil from coal for lighting in 1846, and he built a plant on Long Island near New York. Kerosene quickly replaced whale oil as the standard lighting fuel in North American homes, which led to the collapse of the whaling industry and the size of the petroleum industry.

4 David A. Fife discovered that the strain of wheat he planted in 1842 was far more immune to rust, smut and frost damage than any other he had seen. Each year as the wheat multiplied, he cared for it, and in 1849 sold 260 bushels of his Red Fife wheat to the Otonabee Agricultural Society to distribute among its members. Until the 1950s, most of the wheat grown in western Canada was of the "Red Fife" variety. In 1904 it was crossed with another strain of wheat at the Central Experimental Farm in Ottawa by Charles Saunders, a native of London, Ont., to produce the early maturing Marquis grain that has became the basic wheat grown in North America.

5 In 1854, Samuel McKeen of Nova Scotia designed an early version of the odometer, a mechanism he attached to the side of a carriage to strike off the miles with the turning of the wheels.

6 The automatic steam-driven foghorn was invented by Robert Foulis of Saint John.

7 In 1857, Professor Thomas Sterry Hunt of McGill University was studying chromium-containing minerals, and developed a green ink that could not be destroyed by an acid, a base or any other agent. Hunt sold his invention to the US government for much less than it was worth, and his ink led to the nickname "greenbacks" for American currency.

8 In 1868, John Forbes, foreman of the Starr Manufacturing Company in Dartmouth, Nova Scotia, and his assistant Thomas Bateman, patented a self-fastening skate that attached tightly to a skater's boot with a mechanical lever. The Starr "Acme Club" spring skates met with instant approval and became the world's favourite. They revolutionized figure skating and hockey by allowing quicker starts and stops than the older block skates.

9 Elijah McCoy, the son of former slaves, was born in Colchester, Ontario, on May 2, 1844. Educated in Scotland as a mechanical engineer, Elijah McCoy returned to Canada and got a job as a locomotive fireman/oilman for the Michigan Central Railroad. McCoy identified new ways to lubricate engines to prevent overheating and developed over 80 patents. Machinists and engineers who wanted genuine McCoy lubricators originated the term "The Real McCoy." McCoy went on to invent and market 57 different kinds of devices and machine parts, including an ironing board and a lawn sprinkler.

10 In 1874, Henry Woodward, a medical student from Toronto, patented the first incandescent lamp with an electric light bulb. Henry sold a share of his patent to Thomas Edison, who then came up with a more practical lamp that efficiently transmitted electricity into the light bulb.

11 Although he said he developed the idea for the telephone in Brantford, Ontario, Alexander Graham Bell actually built the first telephone in Boston, Massachusetts, in 1875. However in 1876, he made the first long-distance call over telegraph wires from his home in Brantford to Mount Pleasant, three kilometres away.

12 Canadian railway engineer Sandford Fleming (1827–1915) is the inventor of the world system of time zones. Until about 100 years ago most towns reckoned local noon when the sun was directly overhead, and a train traveller could leave Montreal at 12:00 noon and get to Kingston at 11:53 a.m. In order to clean up railway timetables, on February 8, 1879, Fleming proposed to the Canadian Institute for the Advancement of Scientific Knowledge in Toronto that the world be divided into 24 equal time zones, with a "Standard Time" in each zone, and with Greenwich, England, as the "prime meridian" (the base for calculations). On November 18, 1883, all the North American railway companies adopted his idea. A year later, at a conference in Washington, DC, 25 countries adopted the Fleming proposition, and on January 1, 1885, Greenwich Mean Time (GMT) was established as the basis of his system.

13 At age 19, Thomas Leopold Willson (1860–1915) developed an arc lamp street-lighting system, but it didn't sell, so he turned his attention to trying to make synthetic diamonds from an electric-arc furnace. This didn't work. But in 1892, while attempting to find a way to make cheap aluminum, he produced a crystalline substance that, when dropped in water, emitted a gas that burned with a dark, smoky flame. The substance was carbide, and he had just come up with an affordable means of production, which he sold to Union Carbide in 1896. The gas was acetylene, and Willson set up a company to produce acetylene street lights. But again his street light scheme didn't work—electricity became the preferred method of lighting city streets—so Willson looked for another use for his gas and found it in 1903. His oxyacetylene torch could reach temperatures of 3,300°C, hot enough for welding or to use as a metal-cutting device. The torch was quickly adopted by the automotive and shipbuilding industries, and revolutionized both.

14 Teletype, invented by Frederick George Creed, born in 1871 in Mill Village, Queens County, Nova Scotia. At age 27, working for Western Union in Canso, Nova Scotia, Creed learned Morse code and telegraphy. He soon came up with an idea to interface a typewriter and a telegraphy system to send Morse code, and then to receive the code using the telegraph system and a typewriter in reverse order. In 1889, he set up a company in Glasgow, Scotland, to start manufacturing his Creed Teleprinters, which came to be called the Teletype. In 1898, he demonstrated transmitting the *Glasgow Herald* newspaper to London via telegraphy at a rate of 60 words per minute, and by 1913 his system was routinely used to transmit London newspapers to other major centres in Great Britain and Europe. Creed Teleprinters

were sold around the world, and provided almost instant printed communications between heads of state. In 1923, he showed that his system could also be used for ship-to-shore distress calls, and it became a valuable life-saving system. Frederick Creed died in London in 1957.

15 In the early 1900s, a Toronto chemist and pharmacist named John J. McLaughlin started to bottle soda water. Experimenting with different flavours, he came up with a ginger-flavoured version he called McLaughlin Belfast Style Ginger Ale. He also produced a Pale Dry Ginger Ale and gave it a label with a beaver perched atop a map of Canada. In 1907, he trademarked this version as "Canada Dry Ginger Ale," renamed his company with the same name and soon began bottling "the champagne of ginger ales" at a plant in Toronto. Today, Canada Dry is sold in 90 countries around the world.

16 Peter Robertson patented his square-headed driver and screw system—with green, red and black drivers for the smallest to largest square-headed screws—in 1908. Robertson invented the system after slashing himself badly with a slot-headed screwdriver. The Fisher Body Company (builders of the Ford Model T) soon picked up his invention for their production line. Today, 85 per cent of the screws sold in Canada use the Robertson head, but only 10 per cent of the screws sold in the USA are Robertsons. Speaking of screws, the Interchangeable-Head Screwdriver, with its pop-top handle opening to reveal a collection of five or six of your favourite bits, was patented in 1965 by Waterloo, Ontario's George H. Cluthe.

17 Plexiglas, also called Perspex or Lucite, was patented in 1931 by William Chalmers, a graduate student at McGill University. Chalmers was the first to make a clear, workable acrylic instead of the smoky, opaque material produced to date. He sold his invention to Imperial Chemical Industries, and in 1936, ICI granted a licence to DuPont to produce the material commercially. Today, you'll find it in car tail lights, airplane windshields and safety glasses.

18 Norman Breakley invented the paint roller in 1940, and brought in the era of do-it-yourself home decorating. While his idea was great, his patents were not. He lacked the financial backing to defend his invention against slight modifications and minor infringements, and finally gave up fighting. Other Breakley inventions include a device for tapping beer kegs and a supermarket inventory system.

19 Alexander Graham Bell and Toronto engineer Casey Baldwin invented the hydrofoil in 1908. Their hydrofoil boat *Dhonnas Beag* (Little Devil) or Hydrodome #4 (HD4) held the world speed record of 114 kilometres per hour (70.86 mph) from 1919 until 1929.

20 In 1915 at Ypres, the German army sent clouds of green chlorine and deadly yellow mustard gas toward the Allied-held front lines. Canadian Army physician Dr. Cluny McPherson quickly improvised gas masks made of metal and impregnated cloth to save men from breathing the fumes. He later worked at perfecting this lifesaver, and eventually McPherson's mask became the standard issued to all Allied soldiers. After the war, McPherson masks were used in Canadian mines and chemical plants, cutting exposure to toxic fumes and coal dust.

21 The patent rights for the manufacture of insulin were assigned to the Medical Research Council of Canada by its discoverer, Dr. Frederick Banting.

22 In 1926, four years after inventing his first motorized snow vehicle, Bombardier opened his own garage and kept tinkering with all kinds of equipment and machinery. In 1935 during a blizzard, his 2-year-old child died of appendicitis because snowed-in roads kept him from getting the boy to the nearest hospital, 50 kilometres away. Two years later Bombardier had built and patented a tracked van that held seven people and cost about $7,500. He sold 50 models. In 1958, the inventor found a lightweight two-stroke single-cylinder engine called the Rotax and, in 1959, made 250 snowmobiles he called Ski-Dogs—a typographical error in the literature changed the name to Ski-Doo. A decade later, sales rose to almost a quarter of a million machines a year.

23 Sir William Stephenson of Manitoba, "the man called Intrepid," invented the wire photo, which allowed pictures to be transmitted by wire. Stephenson's first photograph by wire was sent from Washington to Baltimore in a 1923 test. The first transatlantic radiophoto relay came in 1924 when the Radio Corporation of America beamed a picture of Charles Evans Hughes from London to New York. RCA inaugurated regular radiophoto service in 1926.

24 The snow blower was invented by Arthur Sicard in Montreal in 1925.

25 The first electric organ was invented by Morse Robb of Belleville, Ontario.

26 Pablum was invented in the late 1920s in a laboratory at Toronto's Hospital for Sick Children by Dr. Alan Brown, with the assistance of research doctors Theodore Drake and Fred Tisdall. The doctors wanted to help parents feed their babies a nutritious breakfast, so they concocted the first precooked cereal for babies, a blend of alfalfa, wheat meal, oatmeal, cornmeal, wheat germ, bone meal and dried brewer's yeast.

27 F.C.P. Henroteau of Ottawa received the first patent for the modern television camera in 1934.

28 Eli Franklin Burton and a team of physicists that included Cecil Hall, James Hillier and Albert Prebus developed the first practical electron microscope in 1937.

29 In the late 1930s, Dr. Wilbur Franks at the University of Toronto developed the Franks Anti-Gravity G-suit, which he perfected in 1939. The pressure suit counteracted the high centrifugal forces felt by fighter pilots in dog fights, and let them carry out high-speed manoeuvres without blacking out. Used by Allied pilots from 1942 on, it led to the development of the modern space suit worn by astronauts.

30 National Research Council scientist Hugh Le Caine, who built his first musical instrument at age four, built the world's first voltage-controlled music synthesizer in 1945. He also composed unique works that helped popularize electronic music. "Dripsody," a composition produced through the electronic manipulation of the sound of a single drop of water, is considered to be a classic of the genre and the most-played example of this type of electronic music.

31 Winnipeg inventor Harry Wasylyk's polyethylene garbage bag became commercially available in 1969 and it revolutionized the garbage industry. Produced by Union Carbide, the bag was fully endorsed by the Man from Glad.

32 Winnipeg native Dr. John A. Hopps invented the first heart pacemaker in 1950 in a National Research Council lab in Ottawa. While using radio-frequency heating to restore body temperature, he made an unexpected discovery: if a heart stopped beating due to cooling, it could be started again by mechanical or electric stimulation. His first device was too large to be implanted in humans, but the technology was reduced in size, and the first pacemaker was implanted in a human body in 1958. In 1977, Hopps himself was fitted with the device.

33 In 1961 Dr. Edward Asselbergs and his team from the Department of Agriculture accidentally discovered how to make instant mashed potatoes when they were trying to produce instant meat, fish or cheese. They found that adding powdered mashed potatoes kept the dried food from lumping together. And the potatoes didn't taste too bad themselves, either.

34 Nestor Burtnyk and Marceli Wein developed computer animation. In the 1970s, the two NRC scientists invented key frame animation, the basic algorithm for computer animation, which ended the need for an animator to draw each and every frame. The artist simply designates a beginning and end point in movement and computerized logic fills in the intermediate steps. This technology led to the development of a multi-million-dollar Canadian animation industry. By the mid-1980s, three of the world's five major computer animation companies were Canadian. Today, the three companies—Alias, SoftImage and Vertigo—although still located in Canada, are American-owned.

35 Journalists Chris Haney and Scott Abott conceived the game in a bar in Montreal on December 5, 1979. It hit the market in 1982, and by the mid-1990s Trivial Pursuit had sold more than 60 million copies, making it by far the most popular board game in the world. Today, there are 100 versions of the game, and it's sold in 30 countries outside North America and in 16 languages.

36 The programming language Java was invented by James Gosling of Calgary when he was working at Sun Microsystems in 1994.

37 University of Toronto chemistry professor James Guillet and British researcher Harvey Troth received the one-millionth Canadian patent in 1976 for their biodegradable plastic that turns to dust when continually exposed to sunlight.

38 No contest. He's Reginald Aubrey Fessenden (1866–1932), a physicist and the father of radio and TV broadcasting by airwaves. He registered over 500 patents in his lifetime. Fessenden was born the eldest son of the Reverend Elisha Joseph Fessenden and his wife Clementina in East Bolton, Quebec, on October 6, 1866. His boyhood years were spent in Ontario—in Fergus (north of Guelph) and later in Niagara Falls. As a child, he and his uncle watched the Bell family conduct their telephone experiments, and he wondered why Alexander Graham Bell had to use wires, when all you had to do was send waves through the air. In school Fessenden showed an aptitude in mathematics far beyond his years. His boyhood dream was to transmit the sound of the human voice without wires, which he accomplished at age 33 in December 1900, one year before Marconi's efforts at Signal Hill, Newfoundland. Reginald Fessenden died in his house by the sea in Bermuda on July 22, 1932. In the stone of a snow-white memorial above his vault in St. Mark's Church Cemetery, Bermuda, are inscribed the words: "His mind illuminated the past / And the future / And wrought greatly / For the present."

39 Canadian Reginald Fessenden started work for Thomas Edison as a machine tester at age 20 and became his chief chemist by age 24. Fessenden improved the insulation of Edison's bulbs so they were far more efficient. But when financial difficulties forced Edison to lay him off, Fessenden found work with George Westinghouse, and his big breakthrough led to developing light bulbs as a mass product. Edison's method of using platinum connecting wires for an electric lamp made light bulbs very expensive. Fessenden found a much cheaper way, by fusing wires of iron or nickel alloys to the glass. As a result, Westinghouse was able to win the contract to light the 1892 Columbian Exposition in Chicago. By 1901, Fessenden held nine major patents for incandescent lamps.

40 Guglielmo Marconi has been proclaimed the "father of wireless" (even though Alexander Popov and Oliver Lodge were first in the field). Marconi and his employees thought that a spark was essential for wireless broadcasting, and actively pursued the spark method from 1895 until about 1912. His transmission towers were essentially giant spark plugs. But as early as 1898, Reginald Fessenden saw that generating a continuous wave or sustained oscillation was the correct approach to create wireless radio. Marconi finally had to admit that Fessenden was right. In 1914 the Marconi Company licensed Fessenden's continuous wave patents from the National Electric Signalling Company (NESCO), which later became the Radio Company of America (RCA). Marconi simply developed and marketed an early form of radio telegraphy.

41 Television broadcasting was invented by Reginald Fessenden and sold to RCA. Apart from his wireless wave generation patents, Fessenden took out a patent in 1927 for the first television receiver. This patent was part of a package of patents acquired by RCA from the Canadian inventor in 1928, which allowed RCA to proceed with the development of television. After settling his legal bills, Fessenden ended up with only $300,000 from the $500,000 RCA agreed to pay, but the US government's Radio Trust later paid Fessenden $2.5 million to recognize his broadcasting technology, which the military used free of charge during and after World War I.

42 All 15 of these inventions were also the brainchildren of Canadian genius Reginald A. Fessenden.

1 Who said "Canada First; Always Canada"?

2 Where can you find the largest library in Canada?

3 The building of the Panama Canal was the largest earth-moving project in the world. The second-largest took place in Canada. What was it?

Niagara Falls

4 Where was Canada's largest recorded earthquake?
A. St. Lawrence valley
B. Queen Charlotte Islands
C. Mackenzie Mountains
D. Newfoundland's Burin Peninsula

5 Where is Canada's largest shopping centre?

6 If you want to go up Toronto's CN Tower on foot, how many steps will you climb?
A. 1,499
B. 1,760
C. 1,899
D. 1,993

7 Who was Cape Breton's most famous female giant?

8 How many litres of water pour over Niagara Falls every second?
A. 1,570,000
B. 15,700,000
C. 157,500,000

9 What Canadian industrial downfall helped the USA put a man on the moon?

10 Centuries ago the Romans took a regular census of the Empire as a way to measure tax resources and manpower for the Roman legions. When was the world's first regular census of an area larger than a city taken in modern times?

A family in New France is counted in an early census.

11 Who was the first Black Canadian to win the Victoria Cross?

12 What Canadian doctor organized the world's first mobile blood transfusion service during the Spanish Civil War and created the first mobile medical service during the Communist Revolution in China?

13 In the summer of 1858, James Miller Williams dug the first commercial oil well in North America—if not the world—in a tar pit at Oil Springs in Lambton County, in southwestern Ontario. Where was the world's first oil-well gusher?

14 The chefs at which Canadian hotel were the first to cook dinner on an all-electric stove?

15 The world's longest race took place in Canada in what year?

16 Where in Canada would you go to find the world's largest frog?

NAC

James M. Williams

17 Where was the largest non-nuclear man-made explosion in the world detonated?

18 What nineteenth-century Canadian was the world's tallest-known man at 2 metres, 26 centimetres (7 ft., 9 in.)?

19 Who was the first woman in Canada to receive a university degree?

20 Who was the first Canadian woman licensed as a medical doctor?

21 Who was Canada's first female war correspondent?
A. Nellie Bly
B. Kit Coleman
C. Cora Hind
D. Susanna Moodie

22 Which province was first to grant women the right to vote?

23 Elizabeth Smellie became Canada's first female colonel during World War II. She was previously director of which organization?
A. Canadian Red Cross
B. Victorian Order of Nurses
C. Dominion Women's Enfranchisement Association
D. Women's Institute

24 Name the first female combat soldier in the Canadian Armed Forces.

25 What is Canada's first World Heritage Site, the first of 12 such Canadian sites on the list?

Confederation Life

Printing of Canada's first regular newspaper.

32 Who built the first truly sea-to-sea Canadian railway system?
A. Canadian National
B. Grand Trunk
C. Canadian Pacific
D. Ontario Northland

33 In 1906, Toronto's first movie house, The Theatorium, opened on Yonge Street near Queen, and in Montreal, L. Ernest Quimet opened a cinema palace called The Quimetoscope. When and where were the first movies shown in Canada?

26 Name the first regular newspaper published in Canada.

27 Who built North America's first lock canal, and where?

28 What was the first chartered bank in Canada?

29 When was the first Canadian postage stamp issued?

30 When did Canada first adopt the decimal-based coins and currency?

31 The first census of the Dominion of Canada found a population of 3,689,257, including 2,110,502 people of British origin and 1,082,940 people of French descent. When was it taken?

34 When and where did Canada's first symphony orchestra start giving concerts?

35 When was the first Canadian car manufactured?

36 The first Canadian to pilot a powered heavier-than-air machine was Toronto engineer Casey Baldwin, who made the first flight by a

The first airplane flight in Canada.

Canadian in 1908, at Hammondsport, New York. Who made the first airplane flight in Canada?

37 Thomas Wilby and Jack Haney were the first to drive a car across Canada from Halifax, Nova Scotia, to Victoria, British Columbia. When did they accomplish this feat?

38 What was Canada's first feature film, and when did it premiere?

39 When was the first federal income tax charged in Canada and why?

40 Who was the first reigning monarch to visit Canada?

41 Who was the first Royal to set foot on our soil?

42 Which city was the first in Canada to install parking meters?
A. Chicoutimi
B. Sudbury
C. Halifax
D. Windsor

43 What was the first Canadian film to win an Academy Award?

44 When and where did Canada's first drive-in movie theatre open?

45 When and where did Canada's first television station start broadcasting?

46 Who performed Canada's first heart transplant operation and when?

47 What was the name of the first Canadian satellite launched into space?

48 Who was the first Canadian in space?

49

1 Wilfrid Laurier's campaign motto for the 1904 election was "Canada First; Always Canada."

2 The John P. Robarts Library at the University of Toronto, also known as "Fort Book," has over 8,000,000 volumes.

3 The construction of the Red River Floodway was the largest single earth-moving project ever undertaken, apart from the building of the Panama Canal. It is affectionately known as Duff's Ditch, after Manitoba Premier Duff Roblin, and provides a spillway for the Red River around Winnipeg.

4 Canada's largest earthquake was an 8.1 magnitude quake that occurred off the Queen Charlotte Islands in 1949.

5 The West Edmonton Mall in Edmonton, Alberta, has 58 entrances, 800 shops, 20,000 parking spaces and 325,000 light fixtures. It may be the largest shopping mall in the world.

6 The stairs in the CN Tower in Toronto have 1,760 steps. At a height of 553.33 metres (1,815 ft., 5 in.), it is the world's tallest building and free-standing structure.

7 Anna Swan, the famed Giantess of Nova Scotia, weighed 18 pounds when she was born in 1846 and eventually grew to a height of 2 metres, 28 centimetres (7 ft. 6 in.). When she married Martin van Buren Bates (height: about 2 metres, 20 centimetres) in 1880, P.T. Barnum's American Museum in New York proclaimed them the world's tallest couple.

8 Almost 157,500,000 litres of water pour over Niagara Falls each second—that's nine billion litres a minute, the drainage from the entire Great Lakes watershed above Lake Ontario.

9 The first flight of the advanced Avro Arrow took place on March 25, 1968, but less than a year later the government of John Diefenbaker cancelled the order, citing cost and the government's feeling that the fighter was obsolete. The six remaining Arrow prototypes were put to the torch, and the Avro plant in Malton was closed down. Most of Avro's research team dispersed to other companies and occupations, and many of the brightest quickly found work on NASA's Saturn program at Huntsville, Alabama; Cape Canaveral, Florida; and Houston, Texas.

10 The first large census of modern times was Jean Talon's census of New France in 1666. It reported the  population of New France as 3,215 individuals, exclusive of Native peoples: 2,034 men, 1,181 women, and 528 married couples. Talon's first census listed details of age, sex, marital status and occupation. The second census, taken on July 17, 1673, showed a population of 6,705; in 1739, the population was 42,701.

11 Nova Scotia seaman William Hall (1838–1904) was the second Canadian to win the Victoria Cross, for heroism during the Indian Mutiny in 1857. He was also the first man of African descent in the British Empire to win the award.

12 Doctor Norman Bethune organized the world's first mobile medical services.

13 The world's first gusher was also at Oil Springs, Ontario. In July 1861, a driller named Hugh Nixon Shaw reached limestone at 15 metres down. He started drilling further into the rock but was nearly broke and ready to give up at 48 metres when suddenly, on January 16, 1862, there was a loud crack, and then a roar as a black fountain of oil shot out of the well up to tree-top level, splintering his drilling rig and

blackening the grass all around. For 50 days the well gushed out of control, spewing 2,000 barrels a day until Shaw got it under control by extending the pipe six metres above the well and stuffing a weighted leather bag down the bore hole. About 10 million barrels of oil have been removed from the area, and over 25,000 barrels of oil a year are still extracted.

14 Chefs at the Windsor Hotel in Ottawa were the first to cook dinner on an electric stove on August 29, 1883, using an electric range invented by Thomas Ahearn, head of the Ottawa Street Railway Company.

15 The Trans Canada Trail Relay ended in Ottawa on September 9, 2000, and was the world's longest race. The race included bicycles, Rollerblades, horses, cross-country skis, dogsleds and snowmobiles. The world's longest race by water was the 1967 Centennial Voyageur Canoe Pageant and Race from Rocky Mountain House, Alberta, to Montreal, at 5,283 kilometres (3,283 mi.) long. The race took place from May 24 to September 4, and was won by the province of Manitoba canoe *Radisson*, which holds the world record in distance and event time.

16 One New Brunswick bullfrog weighed in at almost 21 kilograms (46 lbs), almost three times the weight of a skunk.

17 The largest deliberate man-made explosion, apart from nuclear detonations, was detonated underwater at Ripple Rock, south of Victoria, BC, in the Strait of Juan de Fuca. This 1958 explosion removed a notorious obstacle from an important shipping lane.

18 The Cape Breton Giant Angus MacAskill, who died at the age of 37 in 1863, was the world's tallest man at the time. He wore size 18 boots. Guinness says the current tallest man in the world is Robert Wadlow, at 8 ft. 11 in.

19 Grace Annie Lockhart graduated from Mount Allison University in 1875, the first woman in Canada to receive a university degree.

20 Jennie Kidd Trout became Canada's first licensed woman physician in 1875.

21 In 1898 Kit Coleman covered the Spanish-American War for a Toronto newspaper. She was Canada's first female war correspondent.

CANADA FIRST AND BESTS

22 Manitoba granted women the right to vote in 1916, the first Canadian province to do so.

23 Canada's first female colonel was also the director of the Victorian Order of Nurses.

24 Heather Erxleben became the first female combat soldier in the Canadian Armed Forces in 1989.

25 On July 11, 1980, the United Nations Educational, Scientific and Cultural Organization (UNESCO) unveiled a plaque at L'Anse aux Meadows, Newfoundland, declaring the Viking ruins a World Heritage Site. It was here that the remains of a 1,000-year-old Viking colony were first excavated in 1960 by Norwegian archaeologists Helge Ingstad and Anne Stine Ingstad.

26 Canada's first newspaper was the *Halifax Gazette*, first published in 1752 by John Bushell.

27 The first canal using locks was built by Captain William Twiss in 1781 at Coteau du Lac, on the St. Lawrence River west of Montreal, to move military supplies up the St. Lawrence.

28 The Bank of New Brunswick, established at Saint John in 1820.

29 April 23, 1851; the red three-penny beaver stamp was designed by Sandford Fleming.

30 Canada adopted a decimal-based currency in 1858.

31 The first census of the Dominion of Canada was taken on April 2, 1871.

32 Canadian Pacific. After a false start in 1872–83, the Canadian Pacific Railway contract received Royal Assent in 1881, and the company started building its prairie section of track. On June 20, 1886, the first Pacific Express left Montreal's Dalhousie Square Station with 170 passengers in two immigrant sleeping coaches, two first class coaches and two first class sleeping coaches (named Yokohama and Honolulu); it also had one dining car (Holyrood), two baggage cars and a mail car. The 4,650-km trip took almost six days to reach Port Moody, British Columbia, the western terminus. In 1889, the first CPR train beyond Montreal arrived in the ice-free port of Saint John, New Brunswick, marking the completion of Canadian Pacific as a coast-to-coast, all-weather railway.

33 On July 21, 1896, John C. Green gave the first display of Thomas Edison's Vitascope at the Ottawa Electric Railway Company's West End Park near the intersection of Holland Avenue and Carling Avenue in Ottawa. This was Canada's first motion picture showing. Two years later, in the fall of 1898, John Schulberg bought an Edison kinetograph and ran a 30-minute show in an empty storeroom on Cordova Street, Vancouver.

34 Canada's first symphony orchestra started giving concerts at Quebec City in 1902.

35 The first true Canadian car, the LeRoy, was produced in 1902, by carriage makers Milton and Nelson Good in Berlin, Ontario, now Kitchener. Their first car is on display at the Doon Heritage Crossroads Museum in Kitchener. Canada's first gasoline service station was not set up until 1908 in Vancouver.

36 In 1909 J.A.D. McCurdy piloted the first flight in the British Empire, at Baddeck, Nova Scotia. McCurdy flew his Silver Dart airplane at an altitude of about 10 metres for nearly one kilometre across Baddeck Bay. Alexander Graham Bell's Aerial Experiment Association (AEA) made the Silver Dart from steel tube, bamboo, friction tape, wire and wood, and covered it with rubberized silk balloon-cloth; power was supplied by the first Curtiss-designed water-cooled engine.

37 On October 12, 1912, Wilby and Haney reached Victoria, after crossing Canada in their REO Special, and dipped the car's wheels in the Pacific. The trip took 52 days, with 41 days of actual driving. Jack Haney was an REO Motor Car Company mechanic from Indiana, Thomas Wilby an English journalist who had previously crossed 14,400 kilometres of US roads in 105 days. Wilby later wrote *A Motor Tour Through Canada*. He went on to work at the *Christian Science Monitor* in Boston. Haney opened his own garage in St. Catharines, Ontario, and later helped develop the Niagara Falls airport.

38 Canada's first feature film, *Evangeline*, premiered in Halifax in 1913.

39 On July 25, 1917, during World War I, Finance Minister Sir Thomas White introduced the Income Tax War Bill in Parliament as a proposal to levy the first national tax on personal income on Canadians; this was to be a temporary wartime measure only.

40 George VI visited Canada in 1939, the first reigning monarch to do so.

41 William IV. In June, 1786 the young Prince William, captain of HMS *Pegasus*, landed on the coast of Newfoundland. The Prince went on to visit Halifax on October 10 before sailing to warmer waters in the West Indies. One year later, in October 1787, His Royal Highness again visited Halifax, staying there until November 11.

42 Sudbury was the first in Canada to install parking meters in 1940, only five years after the world's first parking meters were installed in Oklahoma City on July 16, 1935.

43 The National Film Board documentary *Churchill's Island* was the first Canadian film to win an Academy Award, in 1941.

44 Canada's first drive-in movie theatre opened outside Hamilton, Ontario, in 1946.

45 Canada's first TV station, CBFT Montreal, started transmitting its signal in 1952. The first privately owned TV station began broadcasting in Sudbury, Ontario, in 1953.

46 Dr. Pierre Grondin performed Canada's first heart transplant operation at the Montreal Heart Institute in 1968.

47 Alouette I, the first Canadian-built satellite, was launched into orbit on September 29, 1962. The satellite was used to study the ionosphere from the top down to learn its effect on radio transmissions.

Alouette II followed in 1965, ISIS (International Satellite for Ionosphere Studies) in 1969 and ISIS II in 1971. By 1990, more than 1,000 papers and reports had been published from information received from the Alouette/ISIS Program, initiated in 1958 by Dr. John H. Chapman, director of the Defence Research Telecommunications Agency.

48 Canada's first astronauts were chosen in 1983, including Marc Garneau, Canada's first man in space in 1984, and Roberta Bondar, Canada's first woman in space.

Sports?

1 Who said, "Golf is the favourite game in Scotland. It is played everywhere. It is too slow a game, however, for Canada. We would go to sleep over it"?

2 What is the oldest golf club in North America?

3 When was the Canadian Professional Golfers Association founded?

4 Golf great Arnold Palmer amassed 92 championships in pro competition up to the end of 1993. Where and when was his first professional golf victory?

5 On December 21, 1891, in Spring-field, Massachusetts, James Naismith, a 30-year-old YMCA trainer from Almonte, Ontario, nailed two peach baskets up on opposite ends of the YMCA Training College gym and

James Naismith, 1861–1939

instructed his 18 students to toss soccer balls into them, thus inventing the game of basketball. Why?

6 In 1914, Percy Page formed a women's basketball team from the girls' team of McDougall Commercial High School in Edmonton where he was a teacher. This team held the world senior women's title for 17 consecutive years. What was the name of the team and when did they win Olympic gold for Canada?

7 On November 17, 1968, Al Balding and George Knudson won the World Cup golf tournament in Rome, beating 41 other national teams. What was remarkable about the feat?

8 Which golfer sold shares in himself and his winnings to caddies in order to have enough money to enter the Alberta Open?

9 Which golfer tied for second place at the US Masters in 1969 and won more PGA tournaments than any other Canadian?

10 In her 1968 rookie year, which Oakville, Ontario, golfer was the first Canadian woman to play on the US LPGA tour and beat Kathy Whitworth in a playoff to win the LPGA championship?

11 On July 11, 1990, a gun battle broke out and a policeman was killed over ownership of a golf course. Who did the firing?

12 Who designed the course at the Glen Abbey Golf Club?

13 Where was Canada's only indoor velodrome?

14 Name the French architect of the Olympic Stadium in Montreal.

15 What Canadian was the tennis-playing daughter of a well-known publisher, former Canadian Davis Cup player and minority owner of the Toronto Maple Leafs?

The winning women's basketball team coached by Percy Page.

16 Name the Montreal-born tennis champion who emigrated to England and became top seed in his adopted country.

CP

Winner of six Canadian Junior Tennis titles from 1985–90.

17 What sport in Canada was dominated by the name "Kahn" from the 1950s to the 1980s?

18 With which national team is coach Jack Donohue associated?

19 What is Mike Weir's home town, and what did he accomplish on September 5, 1999, by winning the Air Canada Championship?

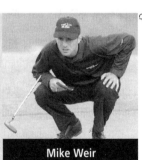

CP

Mike Weir

20 Name the woman who is the only golfer to have won the Canadian, United States, British and Australian amateur championships.

21 What happened in Canadian basketball history on May 22, 1994?

22 Who is the Montreal Canadiens star who in 1950 was voted the best Canadian lacrosse player of the half century?

Lacrosse played on ice, 1883.

NAC

23 What type of motor race is held between Winnipeg and St. Paul, Minnesota, each January?

24 Which sport is the most popular with Canadians over 15 years old?
A. Baseball
B. Curling
C. Golf
D. Hockey
E. Swimming

25 What Calgary family is known for its professional wrestling prowess?

26 The Minto and the Mann Cups are awarded for what sport, and who donated them?

27 Name the Toronto inventor of five-pin bowling.

28 What Canadian sport is called birling?

29 What sport was called baggataway when it was first played in Canada?
A. Cricket
B. Curling
C. Lacrosse
D. Rugby

30 Name the Canadian horse-racing event that was first run in 1859.

31 Which sport was first introduced 75 years ago at the 1923 Calgary Stampede?
A. Barrel racing
B. Bullriding
C. Chuckwagon racing
D. Wild horse breaking

1 John B. Maclean, founder of *Maclean's Magazine*, said in 1891 that golf was too slow for Canadians.

2 The Royal Montreal Golf Club, founded in 1873 by Alexander Dennistown. The Club was also the first to receive the "Royal" prefix (1884); the first to import an English golf professional (William Davis in 1881); the first in North America to allow women members (1891); and the first to play host to the Canadian Open (in 1904).

3 The Canadian Professional Golfers Association was founded in 1911, at Toronto, Ontario, five years before the founding of the US PGA. The Royal Canadian Golf Association (RCGA) and the Canadian Amateur Championship were founded earlier, in 1895.

4 Arnold Palmer won his first professional golf victory at the 1955 Canadian Open, where he had an amazing 72-hole score of 265 (64-67-64-70) at the Weston Golf & Country Club outside Toronto.

5 Dr. Luther Gulick, head of the Phys. Ed. department at the YMCA Training College in Springfield, Massachusetts, asked James Naismith to devise a good indoor phys. ed. activity free of rough play for the football and lacrosse players during the winter season. In response, Naismith invented basketball. Apparently, bodybuilding and calisthenics were becoming boring, and Gulick wanted to eliminate the students' boredom and heighten class morale. Naismith's first basketball teams had nine players each: a goalkeeper, two guards, three centres, two wings and a home man. His first game ended in a score of 1–0, but it was a resounding success. Naismith first printed his 13 formal rules in the Springfield College YMCA

newspaper, *The Triangle*, on January 15, 1892. *The Triangle* was distributed to YMCAs throughout the USA, and the game quickly took off. A year later, Lew Allen of Hartford, Connecticut, made cylindrical baskets of heavy woven wire to eliminate the peach baskets, and in 1894 the first true basketballs replaced the heavier soccer balls.

6 The Edmonton Grads women's basketball team won the world senior women's title for 17 consecutive years. In its 25 years, from 1915 to 1940, the team lost only 20 of 522 games and won Olympic gold for Canada in 1924, 1928, 1932 and 1936. Percy Page, who formed the team in 1914, was the Grads' only coach, and later served as Alberta's lieutenant-governor. Said Naismith, "The Grads are the finest basketball team that ever stepped on a floor."

7 When Al Balding and George Knudson won the World Cup golf tournament in 1968, it was the first victory for a Canadian team since Canada donated the Cup. Golfing's World Cup originated when Canadian industrialist John Jay Hopkins donated the Canada Cup for competition among two-man teams of professional golfers representing their countries. The first Canada Cup tournament was held in 1953 at Beaconsfield Golf Club in Montreal. Seven countries were represented. The trophy was renamed the World Cup in 1967. Since 2000, it has been called the EMC World Cup.

8 Pat Fletcher (1916–1985) turned professional in 1936 at the age of 20. He financed his entry to the Alberta Open by selling shares in his winnings to caddies. In 1954 the English-born Fletcher became the first Canadian in 40 years to win the Canadian Open, at Point Grey in Vancouver.

9 George Knudson (1937–1989) won more PGA tournaments than any other Canadian, taking five CPGA titles and eight PGA victories between 1961 and 1972, and winning the 1966 International Trophy at the World Cup.

10 Sandra Post was the first Canadian woman to play on the US LPGA tour, and in 1968 she was both the first rookie and the first foreign player to take the LPGA championship. In 1979, her best season, she took three tournaments, including the Dinah Shore tournament; finished second on the LPGA money list; and won the Lou Marsh trophy as Canadian Athlete of the Year. In her 16-year career, from 1968–83, she won eight official LPGA events, including three majors.

11 Mohawks at Kanesetake, near Oka, Quebec, put up barricades in March to block expansion of a golf course on land they claim was never signed away. Corporal Marcel Lemay, a 31-year-old constable, was killed during the gun battle as 100 members of the Quebec police tried to storm the barricades.

12 Jack Nicklaus designed the Glen Abbey course in Oakville, Ontario.

13 The only indoor cycling velodrome in Canada was the Montreal Biodome in Montreal. It was built for the 1976 Olympics, but was later demolished and turned into a botanical garden.

14 Roger Taillibert's stadium cost over $1 billion, and is known as The Big Owe.

Designed for the 1976 Olympic Games, the *Stade olympique* was not completed on time due to a strike by construction workers. Its 170-metre leaning tower—one foot taller than the Washington Monument and angled at 45 degrees—is the world's tallest inclined structure. Designed to retract the roof, it stood half finished until 1987 when the roof was finally completed. It took another two years before the roof, made from Kevlar™ weighing 50 ton, became retractable. Problems with opening and closing the roof led to its permanent closure. In the spring of 1998, the orange Kevlar roof was removed and a $26-million opaque blue roof replaced it later in the year. In their disastrous 1991 season, the Montreal Expos spent the last month on the road after a concrete chunk fell from Olympic Stadium. They finished last in the National League East.

15 Carling Bassett, the daughter of Susan Carling Bassett and John Bassett. By age 12, she was the best player in Canada and attending the Bollettieri Academy in Florida. She turned pro after winning the 1982 Orange Bowl, and a year later signed a modelling deal with Eileen Ford. In April 1983, after she lost to Chris Evert at the finals of the Amelia Island tournament, Bud Collins interviewed Bassett, then 16. "I didn't know you were this good," he remarked. "Neither did I!" she responded. Bassett later revealed that she was also battling an eating disorder at the time, and anorexia and bulimia took over her life and derailed her career. She is now happily married with three children, and in 2001 was appointed to the Canadian Sports Hall of Fame, the first woman tennis player so honoured.

16 Greg Rusedski became the top-seeded tennis player in England after emigrating from Canada in 1994. He won six Canadian junior titles from 1985–90, turned pro and captured the Wimbledon junior doubles title with Karim Alami. After moving to England, he reached the fourth round of Wimbledon in 1995, became a British citizen and started competing for his new country. In 1997 Rusedski overtook Tim Henman as top seed in England, and in 1998 he broke the world serving-speed record during the semifinals of the ATP Tour event in Indian Wells, hitting a serve of 149 miles per hour (240 kph).

17 Sharif Khan, the eldest son of legendary squash virtuoso Hashim Khan, arrived in Toronto in the 1960s. He became the reigning wizard of squash in North America for almost two decades, winning every major North American tournament and capturing the American Open Championship 12 times. The Pakistan-born Khan won the world doubles title in the 50 plus category in 1994 with partner Craig Wells.

18 In 1972, Jack Donohue became the head coach of the Canadian men's basketball team and, over the next 17 years, he qualified the team for four straight Olympics. At the 1983 World University Games in Edmonton, the Canadian team defeated the United States in the semifinals and Yugoslavia in the finals to capture the gold medal.

19 Golfer Mike Weir was born in Sarnia, Ontario, on May 12, 1970, and grew up in nearby Bright's Grove. His first international victories were at the 1997 BC TEL Pacific Open and Canadian Masters, and he joined the PGA Tour in 1998. Weir's 1999 victory was the first time in seven years that a Canadian won a PGA Tour event, and the first time since Pat

Fletcher won in 1954 that a Canadian won a PGA Tour event on Canadian soil. That year Mike had seven top-10 finishes, including a second-place finish behind Tiger Woods at the Motorola Western Open. Weir has won two other PGA Tour events—the 2000 WGC-American Express Championship ($1 million prize), and the 2001 Tour Championship ($900,000 prize).

20 Marlene Stewart Streit, born in Cereal, Alberta, won the Canadian, United States, British and Australian amateur championships. She also captured 11 Canadian Ladies Open championships during her career. In 1956 she had 34 straight victories.

Marlene Stewart Streit

21 On May 22, 1994, the new Toronto NBA franchise the Raptors unveiled its name and a logo of a basketball-playing dinosaur. On the NBA season's opening night, November 3, 1995, the Raptors played their first game, beating the New Jersey Nets 94–79 at SkyDome. On the same night, the Vancouver Grizzlies, the other Canadian expansion team, thumped the Portland Trail Blazers 92–80 in their first game.

22 Edouard "Newsy" Lalonde (1887–1971), who got his nickname as a reporter for the *Cornwall Freeholder*, was voted the best Canadian lacrosse player of the half century in 1950. He joined the original Montreal Canadiens hockey team in 1910; won the NHL scoring title four times, with 124 goals in 98 games; and was on two Stanley Cup winning teams. Lalonde spent his summers touring the country with various lacrosse clubs until 1928.

23 Every January, a snowmobile race is held between Winnipeg and St. Paul, Minnesota.

24 More Canadians over 15 years old play golf than any other sport.

25 The Harts are Canada's most famous wrestling family. The family began their careers in Calgary Stampede Wrestling. Bret "Hitman" Hart went to the Mount Royal College of Film in Calgary for a year before making the move to professional wrestling. In 1985 he joined the World Wrestling Federation (WWF) with brother-in-law Jim "The Anvil" Neidhart and, as a solo act, he was a nine-time World Title holder. The youngest of the Hart brothers, Owen, was killed on May 23, 1999, when he fell from the rafters in the Kemper Arena in Kansas City.

26 The Minto Cup was given for junior lacrosse supremacy by Governor General Lord Minto; the Mann Cup by Sir Donald Mann, builder of the Canadian Northern Railway. The Mann Cup began as a challenge cup for Senior A lacrosse, and the first recorded winner was the Young Torontos team in 1910. In 1925, the Canadian Lacrosse Association took over the Cup as its championship trophy.

27 Thomas Ryan, owner of the Temperance Street Bowling Club in Toronto, invented five-pin bowling. Ten-pin bowling came to Toronto in 1905, and was a favourite lunchtime recreation. In 1909, to create a faster game, Ryan moved to five smaller pins with a rubber band circling the throat of each pin, and set up a system in which each pin was given a number of points from one to five. The game caught on quickly, and at one time, Toronto had about 120 bowling houses. The largest was Olympia Edward, at 20 Edward Street (now the World's Biggest Bookstore), which had 64 lanes on four floors, and was one of the first to convert to string-pin machines. Half a million Canadians still play the game.

28 Birling is another name for logrolling.

29 Lacrosse was called baggataway by the First Nations peoples who first played the game.

Early lacrosse players, 1844.

30 The Queen's Plate was first run in 1859 at Woodbine racetrack. In July of that year, directors of the Toronto Turf Club received word that Her Majesty Queen Victoria "had been graciously pleased" to grant a plate of 50 guineas "to be run for in Toronto or such other place as Her Majesty might appoint." This gift launched what is today the oldest consecutive thoroughbred horse race in North America.

31 Chuckwagon racing was first introduced at the Calgary Stampede in 1923.

1 Who was the only Canadian-born winner of the world heavyweight boxing championship?

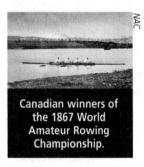

Canadian winners of the 1867 World Amateur Rowing Championship.

2 In 1867, Robert Fulton, George Price, Samuel Hutton and Elijah Ross surprised the favoured European teams by easily winning the World Amateur Rowing Championship at the Paris International Exposition. Where were they from, and what were they known as?

3 Name the Montreal policeman who was widely recognized as the strongest man in the world a century ago.

4 In 1859, a French acrobat was the first to cross Niagara Falls by tightrope. Spectators saw him lower a rope to the *Maid of the Mist*, pull up a bottle of champagne, and sit down while he refreshed himself. He then did a back somersault and recrossed blindfolded, then on a bicycle, then on stilts. Next, he stopped and cooked an omelette in the centre, and then made the trip with his hands and feet manacled. What was his name?

5 What water skier went to his first world championship at age 15 and took 10 Canadian titles from 1965 to 1974?

Canada's best water skier at the World Water Ski Championship, Sherbrooke, Quebec, 1967.

6 What Canadian rower was played by Nicolas Cage in *The Boy in Blue*?

7 What was the name of the first Canadian yacht to compete for the America's Cup sailing title?
A. *Atalanta*
B. *Canada*
C. *Countess of Dufferin*
D. *Great Eastern*

8 Who challenged and beat a horse in a 12-mile endurance race?

The famous Canadian distance runner with his trophies, 1907.

9 Who was the Canadian runner named in 1914 as the "All-round Athletic Champion of the World"?

10 Marilyn Bell crossed Lake Ontario from Youngstown, New York, at the mouth of the Niagara River, to the breakwater at the Canadian National Exhibition in her home town, Toronto, in 20 hours 55 minutes on September 9, 1954, the first person to swim across Lake Ontario. Who did she beat?

13 Who was the first woman to high jump six feet?

The first woman to high jump six feet competing at the Munich Summer Olympics in 1972.

Marilyn Bell

Three of the original Crazy Canucks.

11 Who had his first big marathon win in 1969 at the Fukuoka world championship race in Japan? He won it two more times and also took the Boston Marathon in 1977.

12 How long did it take Ben Johnson to run the 100-metre dash in 1988 (in spite of his Olympic record invalidation)?

14 In the 1970s and 1980s the Canadian Men's Downhill Racing Team were called crazy because they skied at breakneck speeds and appeared to be barely in control. Who were the original Crazy Canucks?

15 If you compete in the Canadian Birkebeiner in Edmonton, what sort of athlete are you?
A. Canoeist
B. Motorcyclist
C. Skier
D. Triathlete

16 Who was the first Canadian to ski to the North Pole and back without support teams or outside help?

63

17 Which member of the Crazy Canucks was not born in Canada?

18 Who invented cross-country skiing?

19 If you "boned an eggplant," what sport would you be participating in?

20 Who wrote, "My glad feet shod with the glittering steel / I was the god of the wingèd heel"?

21 Who was the first athlete ever to complete a quadruple jump in a World Figure Skating competition?

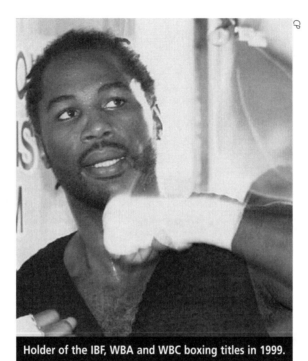

Holder of the IBF, WBA and WBC boxing titles in 1999.

22 What Canadian figure skater won the World, European and Olympic gold medals in the same month?

23 Who was the first Canadian to win the world men's figure skating title?

24 Is the Rideau Canal the world's longest skating rink?

25 What Toronto boxer lasted 15 rounds with champion Muhammad Ali in 1966?

26 What Canadian boxer became the undisputed heavyweight king on November 14, 1999, unifying the IBF, WBA and WBC titles?

27 When Gilles Villeneuve became the first Canadian winner of a Formula One event in 1978, which Grand Prix race did he win?
A. Montreal
B. Belgium
C. Britain
D. Monte Carlo

Gilles Villeneuve driving a Ferrari T4 at the Monaco Grand Prix, 1979.

28 In 1997, Jacques Villeneuve was voted Canada's Male Athlete of the Year. Why?

29 Who was the first Canadian woman to win a cycling world championship gold medal?

30 What Canadian cyclist was unbeatable in bicycle racing in the 1970s, winning gold medals for Canada in the Commonwealth Games and Pan American Games? In 1983, at the peak of his career, he was hit by a truck in the country outside Toronto and paralyzed from the neck down.

31 What was the name of Vancouver's professional North American Soccer League team from 1974 to 1984?

32 What world championship did Cliff Thorburn win in 1980?

33 Which Canadian city has hosted the Pan American games?

34 How many times have the Commonwealth Games been held in Canada?

The jockey who rode Triple Crown winner Count Fleet.

35 Who was the first Canadian named *Sports Illustrated*'s sportsman of the year?
A. Gordie Howe
B. Bobby Orr
C. Ron Turcotte
D. Wayne Gretzky

36 What Canadian horse won the Kentucky Derby in 1964?

37 Name the Canadian jockey who won the Triple Crown riding Count Fleet.
A. Bill Hartack
B. Sandy Hawley
C. Ron Turcotte
D. Johnny Longden

38 What unusual water race starts in Nanaimo every July?

1 Tommy Burns (1881–1955) was the only Canadian and the smallest world heavyweight boxing champion ever, at only 162 lbs and 5'7". He captured the crown from Marvin Hart in Los Angeles on February 23, 1906, and defended his title 11 times within a period of less than two years. He was the first white fighter to agree to a championship bout with a black boxer and in December 1908 lost his title to the legendary black boxer, Jack Johnson.

2 These four rowers were from Saint John, New Brunswick, and as a result of winning the World Amateur Rowing Championship at the 1867 Paris International Exposition, they were known as The Paris Crew. They successfully defended their title against American crews until a British team beat them in 1870. They won a rematch in 1871 but the event was marred by the sudden death of one of the British rowers.

3 Louis Cyr (1863–1912), from Saint-Cyprien-de-Napierville in Quebec, defeated all comers in a North American Open in 1885 and in a world meet in 1892. P.T. Barnum hired him as a strongman, and in Boston, in 1895, Cyr hoisted the heaviest weight ever lifted by a human being: a platform with 19 fat men weighing a total of 1,967 kilograms. On his retirement he opened a tavern in Montreal and amazed the crowds with feats of strength such as resisting the opposing pull of up to four horses.

4 On June 30, 1859, tightrope walker Jean Francois Gravelet (also known as the Great Blondin and the Prince of Manila because he used manila rope) crossed the Niagara Gorge from the USA to Canada several times by tightrope before a crowd of 25,000. On August 19, he crossed pushing a wheelbarrow while carrying his manager

Colcord on his back; a guy rope broke and they were both nearly killed, but Blondin was able to reach the shore in a run.

5 George Athans Jr. (1952–) was Canada's best water skier and was the overall world champion in both 1971 and 1973.

6 Rower Edward "Ned" Hanlan (1855–1908) was single-sculls world champion from 1880 to 1884. He was nicknamed The Boy in Blue and was one of the first rowers to develop and master the sliding-seat technique.

7 In 1876, Alexander Cuthbert's 106-foot *Countess of Dufferin* from Toronto mounted the fourth challenge for the America's Cup, but lost to defender *Madeleine* in the two-race series. This was last time schooners raced for the America's Cup. Cuthbert returned for the next race in 1881 with his 70-foot *Atalanta*, sailing from the Bay of Quinte Yacht Club, but was also dispatched 2–0 by the 68-foot cutter *Mischief*, owned by New York Yacht Club (NYYC) member Joseph Busk of England. The Cup dates from 1851, when *America*, a radically designed black schooner from the NYYC, beat the best British vessels in the Race of Nations around the Isle of Wight for the One Hundred Guinea Cup.

8 Native Canadian runner Tom Longboat (1886–1949), an Onondaga from the Six Nations Reserve near Brantford, beat a horse in a 12-mile endurance race in 1906. In 1907, he was the first Canadian runner to win the Boston Marathon. Longboat competed professionally until 1912 and served with distinction in the Sportsmen's Batallion in World War I.

9 Walter Knox defeated British Empire champion F.R. Cramb and US champion John A. Macdonald in 1914 to take the honour as the all-round athletic champion of the world. In 1909 Canadian Knox had run the 100-yard dash in a world record time of 9.6 seconds.

10 In 1954, the Canadian National Exhibition (CNE) had offered US marathoner and English Channel record holder Florence Chadwick $10,000 if she could swim across Lake Ontario. Chadwick dropped out after several hours with stomach pains and vomiting, and 16-year-old Marilyn Bell emerged triumphantly from the water before a crowd of 50,000 Torontonians at about 8:15 p.m. on September 9, 1954. In 1988, Winnipeg- born Vicki Keith became the first person to swim across all five Great Lakes. She also completed five successful crossings of Lake Ontario, including the only successful two-way swim to date.

11 Jerome Drayton won the world championship marathon three times, the first in Fukuoka, Japan, in 1969. He won the Boston Marathon in 1977 but could only manage a sixth-place finish at the 1976 Montreal Olympics. John Miles was the only other Canadian to win the Boston Marathon, in 1926 and 1929.

12 Ben Johnson ran the 100-metre dash in a world record 9.79 seconds at the 1988 Olympics in Seoul, South Korea, but this time was invalidated by his positive drug test. The Ben Johnson steroid scandal led to the creation of the Dubin Inquiry to examine drug use by athletes in Canada.

13 Canadian Debbie Brill (1953–) was the first woman high jumper to clear six feet in 1971. Her unique jumping style was known as the Brill Bend and helped her take the World Cup in Montreal in 1979 when she beat the world's best high jumpers with a jump of 1.96 metres.

14 The Crazy Canucks of the Canadian Men's Downhill Racing team were "Jungle Jim" Hunter, Ken Read, Steve Podborski, Dave Irwin and Dave Murray. Their aggressive style of racing paid off—they won many medals during the 1970s and 1980s. Dave Irwin, "Ir," as everyone called him, was the wildest, most daring of the Crazy Canucks. He looked like he might also be the best of them when he won a World Cup downhill on a treacherously icy course at Schladming, Austria, in December 1975. But after crashing a few weeks later at Wengen he was unconscious for several hours and was never quite the same again. He spoke more slowly and his speech was sometimes slurred. The two "Daves," Irwin and Murray, retired from the Canadian ski team in 1982, the same year that Steve Podborski became the first non-European to win the men's downhill skiing Féderation Internationale du Ski (FIS) World Cup title. Podborski then put together 23 straight top-four World Cup finishes. "Pod" conquered Wengen and Kitzbuhel as well as many other famous courses and established himself as Canada's first World Cup downhill champion.

15 The Canadian Birkebeiner is a cross-country ski race.

16 On February 13, 1995, at Ward Hunt Island, Nunavut, Richard Weber of Chelsea, Quebec, and Russian MD Mikhail Mlakhov started a 1,500-kilometre ski trek from Canada's northernmost point of land to the North Pole, in a bid to become the first to ski to the Pole and back without support teams or outside help. They succeeded on June 15, and incidentally proved that famous US polar explorer Robert Peary could not have reached the Pole, but rather drifted too far east.

17 Ken Read (1955–) was born November 6 in Ann Arbor, Michigan, where his father was studying medicine. He was raised in Calgary and started competing in ski races at age eight. In 1974, he joined the Canadian national alpine team and in 1975 won the World Cup season opener in Val d'Isère, France, to become the first Canadian male to win a World Cup event. Ken Read won five consecutive Canadian national championships between 1975 and 1980.

18 Cross-country skiing was invented by Herman Smith "Jackrabbit" Johannsen of Norway, who died in 1987—at the age of 102. Born at Horten, Norway, in 1885, he came to Montreal in 1919 as a heavy machinery salesman. In 1932 he settled in Piedmont, Quebec, and started building ski trails throughout the Laurentians. The Jackrabbit Ski League, a cross-country ski program for children, was started in his honour.

19 You can only "bone an eggplant" in snowboarding. Snowboarding has developed its own "lingo" to describe the moves and tricks snowboarders perform. Other snowboarding terms include beat (adj.), bail (v.), bust (v.), chatter (n.), crater (v.), grommet or grom (n.), jib (v.), hucker (n.), fakie (adj.), phat (adj.), stick (v.) and wack (adj.). Ross Rebagliati was the first Canadian and the first person to win an Olympic gold medal in snowboarding.

20 Confederation poet and nature story writer Charles G.D. Roberts penned these lines in his poem "The Skater" in 1896.

21 Kurt Browning was the first to complete a quadruple jump in a World Figure Skating competition in 1988.

22 Barbara Ann Scott (1929–) won her first of two European championship titles in

Stockholm, Sweden, in February 1947, and became the first North American to win that title. In 1948 she won the World, European and Olympic gold medals all in the month of February. Her titles include several

Barbara Ann Scott

North American championships, two European championships, two World championships, and an Olympic gold medal at the fifth Winter Olympic Games in St. Moritz, Switzerland, on February 6, 1948.

23 Donald Jackson was the first Canadian to win the world men's figure skating title in 1962.

24 No. The Rideau Canal runs from Ottawa to Kingston. Only the part inside the city of Ottawa maintained by the National Capital Commission and called the "Rideau Canal Skateway" offers 7.8 kilometres of uninterrupted skating, which is indeed the world's longest skating rink.

25 Canadian challenger George Chuvalo lasted 15 rounds with champion Muhammad Ali in 1966. In 1981, in a 10-round unanimous decision in Nassau, Bahamas, Muhammad Ali lost to Canadian and British Commonwealth heavyweight boxing champion Trevor Berbick.

26 Lennox Lewis became the undisputed heavyweight boxing king in 1999. In 1992, Lewis beat Canadian Donovan "Razor" Ruddock, the man who had swapped punches for 19 rounds with Mike Tyson, to win the WBC version of the heavyweight title. Seven years later he beat Evander Holyfield to take the WBA crown and unify the heavyweight title for the first time since 1992. Lennox Lewis, who was born in England to a Jamaican mother, grew up in Canada. He boxed for Canada at the 1984 Olympics, where he was

beaten in the quarter-finals by eventual gold medallist American Tyrell Biggs, but then won the gold medal in boxing for Canada at the 1988 Olympics in Seoul, South Korea.

27 At the Montreal Grand Prix in 1978 Gilles Villeneuve became the first Canadian winner of a Formula One race. He was born in Berthierville, Quebec, on January 18, 1950, and died on May 8, 1982, in a 250-kilometres-per-hour crash at Zolder, Belgium, while practising for the Belgian Grand Prix. His death led to safety improvements in Formula One cars, and he would not have died had he been driving a modern F1 auto. Villeneuve began his racing career in snowmobiles, and in 1974 won the world championship. He entered his first auto race in 1973 and by 1976 dominated the Formula Atlantic series, winning 9 out of 10 races. Villeneuve then signed with McLaren to drive Formula One, later switching to Ferrari, on whose team he won 6 of the 67 races he drove.

28 Jacques Villeneuve, son of Gilles, was voted Canada's Male Athlete of the Year in 1997 after winning the Formula One Grand Prix driving championship.

29 Tanya Dubnicoff was the 1983 cycling world champion, World Cup winner, three-time Pan Am champion, and had multiple World Cup cycling wins. She was the first Canadian woman to win a cycling world championship gold medal, and in 1993 she won the match-sprint event at the 100th anniversary of the championships at Hamar, Norway.

30 Jocelyn Lovell was Canada's top cyclist in the 1970s and is currently the Canadian co-ordinator for the Spinal Cord Society.

31 The Vancouver soccer team was called the Whitecaps. A new version of the Whitecaps started play in 2001, out of Burnaby's Swangard Stadium.

32 Cliff Thorburn won the World Snooker Championship.

33 Winnipeg has hosted the Pan American games twice: the V Pan American Games, from July 23 to August 6, 1967, was the largest sporting event held in Canada to that date, playing host to 2,361 athletes from 29 countries competing in 18 sports. Winnipeg repeated the feat in 1999, with the XIII Pan American Games, the third largest athletic competition ever held in North America. Winnipeg is one of only three cities in the Americas to have hosted the Pan Am Games more than once.

PAN–AMERICAN GAMES
THE OLYMPICS OF THE WESTERN HEMISPHERE
WINNIPEG CANADA 1967

34 The Commonwealth Games have been held in Canada four times: in Hamilton (1930), Vancouver (1954), Edmonton (1978) and Victoria (1994).

35 Bobby Orr was the first Canadian named sportsman of the year by *Sports Illustrated*.

36 Northern Dancer won the Derby in 1964.

37 Alberta jockey Johnny Longden won the Triple Crown in 1943.

38 The Nanaimo Bathtub Race is run every July. Put on by the Loyal Nanaimo Bathtub Society, the race started in 1967 as the city of Nanaimo's Centennial project. Almost 200 tubbers entered the first competition but only 47 completed the 36-mile course to Vancouver's Fisherman's Cove across the straits of Georgia. Today the race leaves Nanaimo harbour, circles Entrance Island, continues up to and around Winchelsea Island and then heads back to Departure Bay in Nanaimo.

CANADA PLAYS FOOTBALL

1 When did football come to Canada?

2 What was the first Canadian football league?

3 Did Canadians invent American football?

McGill University vs. Harvard University.

4 In 1909, Earl Grey, the Governor General of Canada, donated a trophy for the Rugby Football Championship of Canada, and awarded it personally at the first championship game. The trophy was originally open to competition only for amateur teams that were registered with the Canadian Rugby Football Union. Since 1954, only CFL teams have challenged for the trophy. Which CFL team has won the Grey Cup the most times?

5 What university won the Grey Cup in three consecutive years in the 1920s?

6 What teams played in the first Grey Cup game, and who was the star?

7 Who won the first-ever East-West Grey Cup on December 3, 1921?

8 In what year were the Montreal Alouettes organized and the Regina Roughriders renamed the Saskatchewan Roughriders?

9 When was the first Canadian Football League game played, and what was the score?

10 Which team defeated the BC Lions 18–17 in Vancouver to win the 1983 Grey Cup for their first Grey Cup victory in 31 years?

Toronto quarterback and game MVP after the Argonauts win the 1997 Grey Cup.

11 Name the former Argonauts quarterback who first gained worldwide attention when he won the Heisman Trophy as the best college football player in the USA in 1984.

12 Who was the first player in CFL history to rush for more than 2,000 yards in a season?
A. Eric Blount
B. Kelvin Anderson
C. Willie Burden
D. Mike Pringle

The first Grey Cup game at Varsity Stadium in 1909.

70

13 What is the new name for the reborn Ottawa CFL team, formerly the Rough Riders?

14 Which former premier played as a defensive back for the Edmonton Eskimos in 1949, and what other Alberta premier played for the Esks?

15 What problem caused the 1962 Grey Cup final to be played on two separate days?

16 The Canadian Football Hall of Fame is located in this city.

17 What happened to the Grey Cup in 1970 that had nothing to do with the playing field?

18 Who was the first CFL team to advance to the Grey Cup after a regular-season losing record?

19 What CFL team played their first game on June 10, 1982?

The last Canadian quarterback in the CFL.

20 What quarterback was named Most Valuable Player (MVP) of the CFL three times during the 1960s and, in his final season in 1969, was named both league MVP and top Canadian, as well as Grey Cup MVP? He was the last Canadian quarterback to play in the CFL.

21 Who is the only member of both CFL and US Pro Football halls of fame?

22 What CFL quarterback, nicknamed the Rifle, made the CFL's longest completed pass on record of 109 yards?

23 Name the first and only US-based team to win the Canadian Football League Championship Grey Cup.

24 In what city would you be most likely to hear the cheer "Oskee Wee Wee"?

28 Which quarterback was known as "Old Spaghetti Legs" or "The Fast Freight from Mississippi State"?

29 Which Canadian professional football team was originally a rowing club?

30 These same two teams met in the Grey Cup five times in the 1970s, including for three consecutive years, between 1974 and 1979.

31 What is the name of the Saskatchewan Roughriders' mascot?

25 Named after a Governor General, this trophy represents college football supremacy in Canada.

26 This Senator and Liberal organizer was the commissioner of the CFL for 54 days in 1966.

27 This athlete scored three touchdowns for Toronto in the 1938 Grey Cup final and later became an NHL referee.

1 The first written account of a football game was made on October 10, 1868, by R. Tait Mackenzie, after a game between a team of officers from the English troops garrisoned in Montreal and a team of civilians, mainly from McGill University. The game was played on the downtown cricket grounds in Montreal. It was perhaps the first football game ever played in North America. In 1874, McGill University students devised a set of rules based upon English rugby and took them to the USA.

2 On February 7, 1884, the Canadian Rugby Football Union was formed and the Montreal Foot Ball Club defeated the Toronto Argonauts 30–0 in the first CRFU championship game on November 6.

3 On May 14, 1874 in Cambridge, Massachusetts, Harvard beat McGill University 3–0 in the first game of American/Canadian football, a variation of rugby. The Harvard soccer team had invited McGill's rugby team to play two games—one under Harvard rules, the other under McGill's so-called rugby football rules. The Harvard team was so impressed with the Canadian rules, they passed them on to their brothers at Yale. The first game between Harvard and Yale, using a modified version of the McGill rules, followed later that year. This was also the first game on record where admission was charged for a college football game, and where the football goalpost was also used at both ends of the playing field. Both Canadian and American football evolved from the McGill–Harvard match-ups. The major difference between Canadian and American football is that Canadian football uses a larger field and three downs instead of four.

4 The Toronto Argonauts have 13 Grey Cup victories (1996, 1991, 1983, 1952, 1950, 1947, 1946, 1945, 1938, 1937, 1933, 1921 and 1914), with 11 each for the Edmonton Eskimos and Hamilton Tiger-Cats. Since the Grey Cup was first awarded to the Canadian Rugby Football Union champions in 1909, a team from Toronto has won it on 21 occasions, Hamilton 15 times.

5 The Queen's University Golden Gaels.

6 The original "Big Train," Smirle Lawson (1888–1963) scored two singles and ran 50 yards for a touchdown in the last seconds of the first Grey Cup game to give the Varsity Blues the Dominion championship over Toronto Parkdale, at Varsity Stadium in 1909. Smirle Lawson was captain of the Toronto Argonauts from 1911 to 1914 when he joined the Canadian Expeditionary Force as a medical officer. In 1918 he returned to Toronto and joined the Toronto General Hospital staff; from 1937 to 1962 he was chief coroner of Ontario. The U of T team went on to win the Cup the next two years and again in 1920, following a three-year hiatus as a result of World War I.

7 The Toronto Argonauts beat the Edmonton Eskimos 23–0 before 9,550 fans at Varsity Stadium.

8 In 1946, thanks to the combined efforts of football coach Lew Hayman and businessman Leo Dandurand, the Montreal Alouettes Football Club was founded as the successor to the Montreal Navy and the M.A.A.A. Winged Wheelers, the same year the Regina Roughriders became the Saskatchewan Roughriders. The Alouettes' home was Delorimier Stadium. In 1949, at Toronto's

Varsity Stadium, the Alouettes won their first Grey Cup, defeating the Calgary Stampeders 28–15. In 1955, the Alouettes moved from Delorimier Stadium back to Molson Stadium at McGill University, where the Montreal football team had played before the name of the team changed to the Alouettes.

9 On August 14, 1958, Winnipeg beat Edmonton 29–21 in the first CFL game.

10 The Toronto Argonauts. In 1950, the Argos triumphed in the infamous "Mud Bowl" game, defeating the Winnipeg Blue Bombers 13–0. In 1952, they beat the Edmonton Eskimos 21–11. Then they entered the famous 31-year Argonauts drought, the longest for any modern CFL team.

11 Doug Flutie, six-time CFL Most Valuable Player with the BC Lions (1991), the Calgary Stampeders (1992–94) and the Toronto Argonauts (1996–97). On November 16, 1997, Flutie led the Argonauts to a Grey Cup victory over the Saskatchewan Roughriders 47–23. He also led the Boatmen to the '96 Cup Final over Edmonton 43–37, as well as beating the Winnipeg Blue Bombers 24–10 in the 1992 final as part of the Calgary Stampeders. His eight-year career in the CFL saw him set records for most passing yards, career, with 41,355 yards, as well as 270 touchdowns, putting him fourth on the all-time list. Flutie returned to the NFL in 1998 with Buffalo. In 1998, the first box of "Flutie Flakes" frosted cereal hit the shelves in Buffalo and Boston, with half of the proceeds going to the Doug Flutie, Jr. Foundation for Autism. In 2001 he signed with San Diego.

12 Montreal Alouettes running back Mike Pringle set the CFL landmark in October, 1998, as the first player to gain more than 2,000 yards in a season. Pringle was signed as a free agent by the Alouettes on August 26, 1996.

13 The reborn Ottawa team is the Renegades. In December 2001, the Renegades named Joe Paopao as their new head coach. Paopao was head coach of the BC Lions in 1996, after playing more than a decade in the CFL as a quarterback with the Lions, Saskatchewan Roughriders and Ottawa Rough Riders. The old Rough Riders went into a death spiral beginning in 1991, when the board of directors resigned and the CFL assumed ownership of the club, then sold it to Bernie and Lonnie Glieberman. In 1994 Bruce M. Firestone purchased the club, then sold it a year later to Horn Chen, who folded it after the completion of the 1996 season.

14 Peter Lougheed, premier of Alberta from 1971 to 1985, played defensive back for the Edmonton Eskimos. Another Alberta premier, Don Getty, also played for the Edmonton Eskimos, helping them win two Grey Cup championships. He was the quarterback on the 1956 championship team. In 1959, he was named Outstanding Canadian in the Western Canada Football League and was runner-up for the Schenley Award as Outstanding Player in the CFL.

15 On November 29, 1962, severe lakefront fog at Toronto halted the Grey Cup game between the Hamilton Tiger-Cats and the Winnipeg Blue Bombers with 9:22 left; Bud Grant's Winnipeg team won the Fog Bowl the next day by a score of 28–27.

16 Hamilton is home to the Canadian Football Hall of Fame.

17 The Grey Cup was stolen in December 1969 from the Lansdowne Park offices of the Ottawa Rough Riders, who won it that season. Two months later, Toronto police recovered it from a Toronto hotel locker room after an anonymous tip and returned it to CFL headquarters.

18 In 1981, the Ottawa Rough Riders finished regular-season play with a losing record of 5–11 and then beat the first-place Hamilton Tiger-Cats 17–3 in the Eastern Final to advance to the Grey Cup. Described as the worst team ever to make the playoffs, they put quite a scare into Edmonton by building up a 20–1 halftime lead before losing 26–23 and handing the Eskimos their fourth straight Grey Cup.

19 The Montreal Concordes lost to Toronto in their first game, June 10, 1982. The football team reverted to its former name, the Alouettes, in 1986, and folded in 1987. It was resurrected again when the Baltimore Stallions, granted a CFL franchise on February 17, 1994, relocated to Montreal February 6th, 1996 and chose the name Alouettes. On November 2, 1997, the team left the cavernous Olympic Stadium and moved back to Molson Stadium permanently. On November 26, 2000, the Alouettes played in the Grey Cup for the first time since 1979, losing 28–26 to the BC Lions.

20 Russ Jackson, born in Hamilton in 1936, had a 12-year career with the Ottawa Rough Riders starting in 1958 under Frank Clair. He won the Schenley Award for Most Outstanding Player in 1963, 1966 and 1969—the first Canadian to win the award three times. He also led Ottawa to the Grey Cup in 1960, 1968 and 1969. According to Ottawa sports columnist Eddie MacCabe, "Jackson was perhaps the last of a vanishing breed—the Canadian Quarterback."

21 Harold "Bud" Grant, the only coach to win 100 games in both the CFL and NFL, is the only football player in both the CFL and US Pro Football halls of fame. A member of the 1950 NBA champion Minneapolis Lakers, Grant played football for the Winnipeg Blue Bombers and was a three-time CFL All-Star offensive end, leading Winnipeg to four Grey Cup titles (1958, 1959, 1961, 1962) in six appearances. As coach, he holds the all-time rank of third in CFL wins (122). His Minnesota Vikings lost all four Super Bowl attempts in the 1970s; he holds the all-time rank of eighth in NFL wins.

22 Montreal Alouette Sam Etcheverry (1930–) won the single-season passing mark of 4,723 yards in 1956, with 276 completions in 446 attempts. He completed a 109-yard pass to Hal Patterson against Hamilton on September 22, 1956, at Montreal. In his career he made 1,630 completions from 2,829 passes for 25,582 yards; he had 163 interceptions and 174 touchdowns. He played in three Grey Cup finals and coached the Alouettes to a 1970 Grey Cup victory.

23 The Baltimore Stallions, on November 19, 1995, were the only US-based team to win the Grey Cup. The seven US teams that played in the CFL for a short time in the 1990s were the Baltimore Stallions, Birmingham Barracudas, Las Vegas Posse, Memphis Mad Dogs, Sacramento Goldminers, San Antonio Texans and Shreveport Pirates.

24 "Oskee Wee Wee" is the Hamilton Tiger-Cats cheer.

25 The Vanier Cup was created in 1965 when the late Governor General Georges Vanier granted permission to the Canadian Save the Children Fund to use his name for the trophy awarded to the winner of the annual Canadian College Bowl. For the first two years, the Canadian College Bowl was an invitational event featuring two outstanding Canadian college football teams selected by a national panel, and the Governor General

personally presented the first Vanier Cup to the University of Toronto Blues at Varsity's athletic banquet in the spring of 1966. The following year, the Vanier Cup game was declared the national football championship of the Canadian Intercollegiate Athletic Union, with semifinal playoffs in Atlantic and Western Canada to determine the finalists. In 1982 the name of the National Championship game was changed to the Vanier Cup, Canada's University Football Championship. In 2000, over 18,260 fans attended the 36th annual Vanier Cup, making it the largest single amateur sporting event in Canada that year.

26 Senator Keith Davey, CFL commissioner for 54 days, set in motion several reforms. The recommendations of the Committee On One League (COO) were approved to bring operating matters under control of the League. The Players' Pension Fund was established, and on January 1, 1966, the Canadian Rugby Union (CRU) became the Canadian Amateur Football Association (CAFA), turning over the Grey Cup trophy to the CFL. The CFL League Office took up residence at 11 King Street West in Toronto in the Montreal Trust Building.

27 Red Storey still jointly holds the "Most Touchdowns—One Game" Grey Cup record for his three touchdowns on December 10, 1938.

28 Jackie Parker led the Edmonton Eskimos to three straight Grey Cups in the 1950s and was known as "Old Spaghetti Legs"

or "The Fast Freight from Mississippi State." At the 1954 Grey Cup game, Parker's famous 91-yard fumble return for a touchdown, with time running down and the Alouettes threatening to score, led to punter Bob Dean booting the ball through the uprights to give the Eskimos a one-point cushion and a 26–25 victory. Parker also led the Argos from 1963 to 1965 and the BC Lions from 1966 to 1968. He won the Schenley as the CFL's top player three times, was an All-Star for eight straight years and scored 750 points.

29 The Toronto Argonauts, named for the legendary Greek heros, were originally a rowing club.

30 The Montreal Alouettes and the Edmonton Eskimos. In 1979, at Montreal, Edmonton beat Montreal 17–9; In 1978, at Toronto, Montreal beat Edmonton 20–13; In 1977, at Montreal, Montreal beat Edmonton 41–6; In 1975, at Calgary, Edmonton beat Montreal 9–8; In 1974, at Vancouver, Montreal beat Edmonton 20–7. Also, in 1956, at Toronto, Edmonton beat Montreal 50–27. In 1955, at Vancouver, Edmonton beat Montreal 34–19. In 1954, at Toronto, Edmonton beat Montreal 26–25.

31 Gainer the Gopher is the mascot of the Roughriders.

1 Who did the last-place Pittsburgh Penguins take as their first pick in the 1984 National Hockey League entry draft?

Wayne Gretzky is presented with a record book after setting the NHL record for career goals.

2 On August 14, 1980, 19-year-old Wayne Gretzky was named the National Hockey League's Most Valuable Player. What was remarkable about the feat?

3 In 1952, who scored three goals in 21 seconds for the Chicago Black Hawks?

4 In 1970, who became the first defenceman to win the NHL scoring title?

5 In a 1976 game against the Boston Bruins, he set a single-game scoring record of six goals and four assists. Name this Toronto Maple Leafs player.

6 Who retired as a player at the age of 52 after having scored over 1,000 goals in his professional hockey career?

7 As a rookie, who scored 53 goals for the New York Islanders in the 1977–78 season?

8 On June 27, 2001, the Canadian government unveiled a monument in Jacques-Cartier Park in Hull, Quebec, honouring what famous hockey player?

9 Who asked, "How would you like a job where, every time you make a mistake, a big light flashes on and 15,000 people scream at you?"

10 What important event changed hockey goaltending on the night of November 1, 1959, at New York's Madison Square Garden?

11 This former Montreal defenceman won seven Norris trophies and was selected to the All-Star team 10 times.

12 Who was the 1950s NHL star criticized and traded by his team for trying to launch a players association or union?
A. Doug Harvey
B. Ted Lindsay
C. Red Kelly
D. Tim Horton

13 Who was the first black person to play in the NHL, and when did he first play?

14 The Leaf's Stanley Cup victory in 1964 was noteworthy for the heroics of what player who played with a broken ankle?

15 Who said, "If you can't beat them in the alley, you can't beat them on the ice."

16 After winning the 1972 Canada–Russia series, who said, "I finally realized what democracy was all about"?

17 In 1985 a bronze statue of this former Canadiens goalie was unveiled in St-Laurent, a suburb of Montreal. It shows him standing in his well-known pose, with his arms leaning across his stick, waiting for the action.

18 When was the first women's hockey game in Canada?

19 Who was the first woman to play goalie for an NHL team?

Paul Henderson scores the winning goal for Canada against the U.S.S.R. in 1972.

An early indoor hockey match in Quebec, 1910.

20 Who scored the first regular season goal in NHL history?

21 Who made his first broadcast of a hockey game over telephone wires?

22 When did Toronto win its first Stanley Cup as the Maple Leafs?

23 What team returned to the NHL for the 1992–93 season after a 60-year absence?

24 What was the original name of the Edmonton Oilers?

25 Name the four old divisions in the NHL.

26 What are the rhyming nicknames of the two French brothers who are hockey legends?

27 What NHL player was called the Golden Jet?
A. Gordie Howe
B. Frank Mahovlich
C. Bobby Hull

28 What did Lord Stanley do in 1888?

29 On December 19, 1904, the Klondike Wanderers hockey team started a nine-day walk from Dawson City to get a boat to Seattle to catch a train to Ottawa. Their leader and owner, Toronto-born mining promoter Klondike Joe Boyle (1867–1923), was founder of the Canadian Klondike Mining Company, and in 1911 built the first hydroelectric plant in the Yukon. He was later a spy for British and French oil interests, and the friend and lover of Queen Marie of Romania. Why was this team trying to get to Ottawa?

A turn-of-the-century hockey game at McGill University in Montreal.

30 What teams battled for the very first Stanley Cup in 1893, and who won?

31 Who holds the record for the most goals scored in a single Stanley Cup playoff game?

32 Competing for the Ottawa Senators in a Stanley Cup game, who played every position, including goalie?

33 When did the Vancouver Canucks first make the Stanley Cup finals?

34 The Winnipeg Jets never won the Stanley Cup, but what championship cup did they win?

35 What is the former name of the World Cup of Hockey tournament?

36 Where and when was the first Women's World Hockey Tournament held?

1 Mario Lemieux, now owner of the Pittsburgh Penguins, was their first pick in the 1984 NHL draft. Born in Montreal in 1965, Lemieux dropped out of school at age 16, a year after joining Montreal's Laval Voisins junior hockey team. During his career Lemieux was the NHL Rookie of Year (1985 Calder Memorial Trophy); four-time NHL scoring leader (Art Ross Trophy 1988, 1989, 1992, 1993); and twice the regular season Most Valuable Player (MVP) (Hart Trophy 1988, 1993). He won the 1993 scoring title despite missing 24 games to undergo radiation treatments for Hodgkin's disease. In 1996-97 he played his last season and the Penguins retired his number 66 sweater. Mario Le Magnifique had 613 goals, 881 assists and 1,494 total career points in a span of 12 seasons. No player in history has averaged more goals per game (.823) than Lemieux. In 1997, he acquired his old team for back salary and extras played a few more games and in 2002, captioned Canada's gold medal team at Salt Lake City.

2 Wayne Gretzky was the youngest player ever to win the NHL MVP award when he first received the honour in 1980, and he won it for the next five years in a row. In 1981, Gretzky scored 50 goals in 39 games, a new NHL record. "You miss 100 per cent of the shots you never take," Gretzky once said. He passed his hero Gordie Howe as the National Hockey League's all-time scoring leader, with 1,851 career points, on October 15, 1989, in Edmonton. That day the Los Angeles Kings star got two goals and one assist against his former Oiler teammates. Gretzky did it in his 780th NHL game; Howe's record came in 1,767 games.

3 Bill Mosienko scored three goals in 21 seconds.

4 Bobby Orr was the first defenceman to win the NHL scoring title, with a 33-goal, 120-point season in 1970, the first of six straight years with 100 points or more. In the 1972 NHL playoffs he scored 24 points, a record for a defenceman. Born in Parry Sound, Ontario, in 1948, Orr started skating at age four, was signed by the Boston Bruins at age 14 and had an outstanding junior career with the Oshawa Generals until he joined the Boston Bruins at age 18. He led the NHL in assists five times, won the James Norris Trophy as best defenceman eight years in a row and was regular season MVP three times (1970–72). In 1979 he had to retire with a bad knee, with a career 270 goals and 645 assists; unfortunately, as one of Alan Eagleson's first clients, he suffered financially.

5 Darryl Sittler set this single-game scoring record.

6 Gordie Howe is Floral, Saskatchewan's most famous athlete, and his 32-year career is the longest in NHL history. Howe finished among the top five scorers of the National Hockey League for 20 years straight and was the first player to score 1,000 career major-league goals (1977). He played for the Detroit Red Wings of the NHL (1946–1971); the Houston Aeros of the World Hockey Association (WHA) with his sons Mark and Marty (1973–1977); the New England Whalers of the WHA (1977); and the Hartford Whalers of the NHL (1978–1980). Howe won six NHL scoring titles and was awarded the Hart Trophy as the most valuable player six times. He retired in 1980, at age 52, as the NHL leader in career goals scored with 801. He is second only to Wayne Gretzky on the NHL list for total points scored (goals and assists combined), with 1850.

CANADA PLAYS HOCKEY

7 Mike Bossy scored 53 goals in one season.

8 In 2001, Maurice "Rocket" Richard was honoured with a plaque in Jacques-Cartier Park in Hull, Quebec. He played for the Montreal Canadiens from 1942 to 1960. Born in Montreal, Quebec, Richard was the first to score more than 50 goals in a season (1944–45) and first to score 500 career goals. He led the League in goals five times and played on eight Stanley Cup winners in Montreal. In March 1955, Richard struck Boston's Hal Laycoe with a stick and wrestled off a linesman who tried to intervene. When League president Clarence Campbell suspended Richard for the rest of the season, including the playoffs, Campbell was attacked in the Montreal Forum, and fans rioted through the streets of Montreal. Said Frank Selke, "When Maurice is worked up, his eyes gleam like headlights, not a glow, but a piercing intensity. Goalies have said he's like a car coming at you at night. He is terrifying." Before he died on May 27, 2001, he was honoured by the NHL with a trophy bearing his name that is awarded to the league's top goal scorer each year.

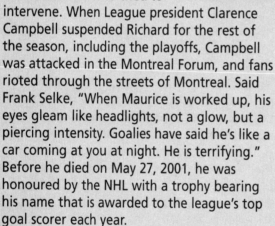

Maurice "Rocket" Richard, 1921–2001

9 Jacques Plante, who played as goalie for the Montreal Canadiens from 1953 to 1963 and helped them win the Stanley Cup six times.

10 Three minutes into the game between the New York Rangers and the Montreal Canadiens, a Ranger slapshot struck Canadien goaltender Jacques Plante in the face and shattered his nose. There was no backup goalie, and it took seven

Jacques Plante, 1952–1975

stitches to close the gash below Plante's nose. The crowd was shocked and surprised when he returned to the ice wearing a face mask he had designed himself out of a welder's mask. The Canadiens won 3–1 that night, and Plante went on to win his fifth straight Vezina Trophy as the NHL's best goalie, helping the Canadiens to their fifth straight Stanley Cup championship that season. Gerry Cheevers, the Boston goalie and later Boston coach, was the first goaltender to paint stitch marks on his mask.

11 Doug Harvey won seven Norris trophies and made the All-Stars 10 times.

12 Ted Lindsay was traded to Chicago by Detroit in 1957 for his efforts to found a players' union. Born in Renfrew, Ontario, on July 29, 1925, "Terrible Ted" Lindsay was, at only 5'8" and 160 pounds, a small player, but he never backed down from a fight, and picked up about 400 stitches on his face during his playing career. After helping the Oshawa Generals win the Memorial Cup in 1944, he made the jump to the Detroit Red Wings at age 19, negotiating some tough clauses into his contract that guaranteed him regular playing time. Playing left wing on Detroit's famous "Production Line" with Gordie Howe and Sid Abel, he helped the Wings win eight regular season titles and four Stanley Cup championships in a 12-year span during the 1940s and 1950s. In 1957, he led the crusade for players' rights, and helped create the first professional hockey players' union, the NHLPA, serving as its first president. He later became Detroit's general manager and was named NHL Executive of the Year in 1978. His number 7 jersey was retired by the Red Wings in 1991.

13 New Brunswick native Bill O'Ree played his first game for the Boston Bruins on a line with Don McKenney and Bronco Horvath in a

3–0 victory over the Montreal Canadiens January 18, 1958. He was the first black player in the NHL.

14 The Leafs were down three games to two when Bob Baun broke his ankle blocking a Gordie Howe slapshot. With his ankle taped up, he scored the overtime goal to win game six and did not miss a shift in the Leafs' game-seven victory two days later. Baun was on crutches for two months, after finally allowing his leg to be put in a cast.

15 Conn Smythe, the founding owner of the Toronto Maple Leafs and builder of Maple Leaf Gardens, quoted in *Maclean's* magazine, January 1, 1952.

16 After scoring the Canada–Russia series-winning goal in Moscow on September 28, 1972, Paul Henderson said, "When I scored that final goal, I finally realized what democracy was all about." He scored three game-winning goals for Team Canada in that famous tournament.

17 A statue of Ken Dryden was erected in Montreal in 1985. Born in Hamilton, Ontario, on August 8, 1947, Ken Dryden was called up to the Canadiens from the Montreal Voyageurs of the AHL in 1970. In the 1970–71 season, he played in only six regular season games, but shone in 20 playoff matches. Dryden's brilliant play won the Canadiens the Stanley Cup and earned him the Conn Smythe Trophy as MVP. Dryden went on to win the Vezina Trophy for best goaltender five times (shared 1977, 1978 and 1979) over his eight NHL seasons until he retired in 1979 to resume his law studies and embark on a legal career. He was appointed Ontario's first Youth Commissioner in 1984 and has written two books on hockey, as well as *In School: Our Kids, Our Teachers, Our Classrooms*. In 1997 he

returned to hockey as the Maple Leafs president and general manager.

18 In 1889 Lady Isobel Stanley and her Government House team played the Rideau Ladies in what may have been the first women's hockey game in Ottawa. In 1900, the first women's ice hockey league was organized with three teams from Montreal, one from Quebec City and another from Trois-Rivières.

19 In 1992, Manon Rhéaume started in a pre-season game for the NHL's Tampa Bay Lightning against the St. Louis Blues. On December 13, 1993, Manon Rhéaume played in goal for the Atlanta Knights of the International Hockey League in Salt Lake City, also becoming the first woman to play goalie in a regularly scheduled professional hockey game.

20 Who scored the first regular season goal in the NHL is a toss-up. On the league's opening night of December 19, 1917, the Quebec Bulldogs' best player Joe Malone joined the Canadiens and scored five goals, including possibly the first goal ever scored in the NHL, as Montreal beat Ottawa 9–4. In the other league game being played in Toronto, Montreal Wanderers Dave Ritchie also scored what may have been the first NHL goal in a 10–9 victory over the Toronto Arenas. This was also the first NHL game played on artificial ice and it was the team's lone victory in the NHL: less than a month later, their arena burned down and they withdrew from the league. Sixteen of the players on that first day wound up in the Hockey Hall of Fame.

21 Foster Hewitt made his first broadcast of a hockey game in 1922.

22 The Maple Leafs won their first Stanley Cup title in their first season in Maple Leaf

Gardens, which opened November 12, 1931. On February 14, 1927, Conn Smythe took over the team previously known as the Toronto St. Patricks and renamed them the Leafs. In the 1930s, because of the Depression, he had to pay workers at the Gardens with shares.

23 In 1992 the Ottawa Senators returned to the NHL after last playing in the 1932–33 season and being sold to a St. Louis group, who renamed them The Eagles. They played poorly their first year, with only 10 wins and 70 losses, but by the end of the 1990s they were again one of the elite teams of the NHL.

24 The Alberta Oilers changed their name to the Edmonton Oilers after the first WHA season. The Oilers played seven seasons in the WHA, reaching the Avco Cup Final in the league's final season of 1978–79, where they lost the best-of-seven series to the Winnipeg Jets in six games. In 1979, owner Peter Pocklington acquired a National Hockey League franchise, and predicted the team would win a Stanley Cup in five years.

25 From 1974–93, the NHL had two "conferences." The Campbell Conference in the south and west had the Patrick division (roughly Atlanta, Calgary, New York and Philadelphia) and the Smythe division (Chicago, Minnesota, St. Louis, Edmonton, Colorado), and the Prince of Wales Conference in the east had the Adams division (Toronto, Boston, Buffalo, Quebec, Minnesota) and the Norris division (Montreal, Detroit, Hartford, Pittsburgh, Washington). Is that perfectly clear?

26 Maurice and Henri Richard were nicknamed the Rocket and the Pocket, respectively.

27 Bobby Hull was nicknamed the Golden Jet. After 15 seasons with the Chicago Blackhawks, Hull shocked the hockey world when he announced in June 1972 that he had signed a 10-year, $2.75-million deal with the WHA's Winnipeg Jets. Hull's jump to the WHA gave the league instant credibility, and changed the hockey pay scale forever. Eventually, Winnipeg entered the NHL, and Hull closed his career in the 1979–80 season with a short stint as a Hartford Whaler playing alongside Gordie Howe.

28 In 1888, Governor General Lord Stanley ordered his staff to create an outdoor skating rink on the grounds of Rideau Hall for his wife and 10 children. Five years later, in 1893, he donated a silver bowl worth about $50 for the top amateur hockey team in Canada.

29 The Klondike Wanderers left Dawson City on December 19, 1904, in order to reach Ottawa for the Stanley Cup tournament on January 13, 1905.

30 The Montreal Amateur Athletics Association defeated the Ottawa Senators in the very first Stanley Cup game in 1893.

31 In January 1905, one-eyed Frank McGee scored 14 goals to lead the Ottawa Silver Seven to a 23–2 win over Dawson City in game two of a two-game total-goals tourney. He still holds the record for the most goals scored in a single Stanley Cup game. Frank McGee was killed in action at the Somme, September 16, 1916.

32 In a 1923 Stanley Cup match, Ottawa Senator Francis King Clancy became the first player to play all six positions. After playing all five skating positions, he guarded the net while goaltender Clint Benedict served a match penalty in the second period. Clancy held the Vancouver Millionaires at bay during his two minute stint in goal. That final also marked the first time that two-sets of

brothers opposed each other—Corb and Cy Denneny and George and Frank Boucher stood on opposite sides of the centre line for the opening face-off. In 1930, Toronto's Conn Smythe bought Clancy from the cash-strapped Senators for $35,000 and two fringe players, and he helped the Leafs win their first Stanley Cup title in 1932.

33 The Vancouver Canucks reached the Stanley Cup finals in 1982 and 1994. The 1982 Canucks took the semifinal against Chicago. This series is remembered for the team being fined for deriding the officials. Coach Roger Neilson waved a white towel derisively at referee Bob Myers, denoting his mock surrender, and Tiger Williams and other Canucks hoisted towels on their hockey sticks and did the same. The white towels didn't work in the next round, as the New York Islanders took their third of four straight Cup titles, four games to zero. In 1994, Vancouver stretched the New York Rangers to the limit before finally bowing in a raucous game seven that rocked Madison Square Garden, ended the Rangers' 54-year Cup drought, and caused a riot in the streets of Vancouver.

34 In the WHA's final season of 1978–79, the Jets won the Avco Cup, beating the Edmonton Oilers in six games.

35 The Canada Cup was founded in 1976 and renamed the World Cup of Hockey in 1996. It was the first international hockey tournament in which professionals were included in the participating national teams of the best hockey countries in the world. Players such as Bobby Hull, Guy Lafleur, Phil Esposito, Bobby Clarke, Darryl Sittler and Gerry Cheevers were on the team representing Canada.

36 The first Women's World Hockey Tournament was held in 1987, at the Centennial Arena in North York, Ontario. Teams from Canada, the USA, Sweden, Switzerland, Holland and Japan competed, and Team Canada won the championship and the first McCallion Cup. The first International Ice Hockey Federation Women's World Championship was in Ottawa in 1990 where Team Canada skated to a 5–2 victory over the US women's team. In Nagano in 1998, women's ice hockey become an Olympic medal sport and the USA won the first gold medal, beating Canada, who had to settle for silver.

1 Who was the first Canadian to win Olympic gold?

2 Who captured the first Olympic gold medal for Canada?

3 Who is the most decorated Canadian Winter Olympian?

4 What Canadian won the marathon at the 1906 interim Olympic Games in Athens, and was joined for the last 50 metres by Prince George of Greece running alongside him?

5 Who was the first Canadian to win two gold medals at an Olympic Games for the 400-metre and 1,500-metre swimming races?

6 What Canadian-born diver won two gold medals and was the first person ever to receive a perfect 10 score?

7 Who was the first Canadian team to win an Olympic hockey gold medal?
A. RCAF Flyers
B. Toronto Granites
C. Winnipeg Falcons
D. Trail Smoke Eaters

8 Who was voted Canada's Female Athlete of the Half Century in 1950, and what Olympic medal did she win?

9 Who is the only Canadian female athlete to have won an individual gold medal in a track and field event at the Olympics?

NAC

Karsh's portrait of Canada's first female Winter Olympic gold medal winner.

10 Who was the first Canadian woman to win a Winter Olympic gold medal?

11 Who won the first Olympic ski medal awarded to a Canadian?

NAC

Female Athlete of the Half Century (second from left) competing in the 100-metres at the VIII Olympiad, 1928.

12 Name the Canadian sculptor who designed the bronze medallion officially adopted as the Olympic Shield at the Tokyo Olympic Games in 1964.

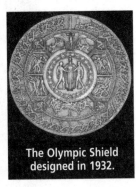

The Olympic Shield designed in 1932.

13 What Canadian runner won silver in the 100-metre sprint at the 1932 Los Angeles Olympics, only to find later that she had been beaten by a man?

14 Canada lost only one basketball game on its way to a silver medal at the 1936 Berlin Olympics. What special person was in the audience for the gold medal game against the USA?

15 At the 1964 Winter Olympics, a team of four Canadians surprised the favoured European teams by winning a gold medal. In what sport? Extra points if you can name the members of the team.

Canadians win gold at the 1964 Winter Olympic Games in Innsbruck, Austria.

16 She won a gold and silver medal for skiing at Grenoble in 1968. What is her name?

17 Who set two world records in the sprint distances of 100 yards and 100 metres and won a bronze medal at the Tokyo Olympics in 1964?

18 What skater was the only medal winner from Canada at the 1972 Sapporo Olympic Games?

Future gold medal skier, racing in Innsbruck, Austria, 1964.

19 At the 1972 Sapporo Olympics in Japan, a 14-year-old Canadian girl was the youngest competitor at the Games. In the 1976 Winter Olympics in Innsbruck, she won the gold medal in giant slalom. What was her name?

20 Who won a bronze medal for figure skating in the 1976 Olympics?

21 On February 18, 1980, at the Lake Placid Olympics, Ken Read's ski came off in the starting gate of the downhill race. Who went on to finish as top Canadian, and became the first Canadian to win an Olympic medal in the event?

Greg Joy at the 1976 Summer Olympics in Montreal.

22 How many gold medals did Canadians win at the 1976 Montreal Olympics?

23 At what Winter Olympics did Canada win its highest medal count?

The first Canadian to win back-to-back gold medals in the same event.

24 What Canadian figure skater won two silver medals in Olympics competition, and was the first person to land a quadruple jump combination— a quadruple toe loop/double toe loop—in competition?

25 Who was the first Canadian athlete to successfully defend her gold medal in an individual Olympic discipline?

27 Clara Hughes won two bronze medals in cycling at the Atlanta Summer Olympics and a bronze in speedskating at the Salt Lake City Winter Olympics, the first Canadian woman to win medals in both summer and winter Olympic games. Who was the first Canadian woman ever to compete in both the Winter Olympics and the Summer Olympics in the same year?

28 What Mohawk athlete held up an eagle feather to honour his grandfather and his Native heritage while being awarded medals at the 1984 Los Angeles Olympics?

26 Name the biathlon athlete who was the first Canadian woman ever to win two Olympic gold medals, and the first non-European to win Olympic biathlon golds.

The Canadian men's hockey team after winning Olympic gold at Salt Lake City, 2002.

29 What is the largest number of medals won by Canada at a single Olympic games?

30 Who was Canada's first female athlete to win two gold medals in one Olympic Games competition?

Canada's first female double-gold winner.

31 At age 19, at the Los Angeles Olympics, this athlete won the bronze medal in the heavyweight rowing doubles sculls; in 1992 she won bronze at Barcelona with a specially fitted brace two months after suffering a broken ankle and ligament damage to the ankle after being rammed while preparing for a regatta in Europe.

32 July 27, 1996, was a day of glory at Atlanta for Canadians. Who won gold medals on that day?

33 What was remarkable about Marnie McBean and Kathleen Heddle's victory at Atlanta?

34 In what city were the yachting events of the 1976 Montreal Olympics held?

35 What caused Canada to join the US boycott of the Moscow Summer Olympics in 1980?

36 Name the sport in the Summer Olympics in which Canadians have won the most gold medals.

37 Who won the first swimming golds for Canada in 72 years at the 1984 Summer Olympics in Los Angeles?

38 What gold-medal swimmer was killed in a car accident outside a Montreal bar on November 28, 1989?

1 George Orton won gold in the 2,500-metre steeplechase at the II Olympiad (1900) in Paris, France. The first Canadian to win Olympic gold, the 27-year-old Strathroy, Ontario, native also finished third in the 400-metre hurdles. In both events he was invited to compete for the Americans, because Canada didn't have an Olympic organizing committee and official team until 1908, and he was a graduate student at the University of Pennsylvania. Athletes were first required to compete as members of national teams at the IV Olympiad in London in 1908.

2 Even though Canada didn't have an Olympic organizing committee and official team, the Winnipeg Shamrocks Lacrosse Club captured Canada's first gold medal at the 1904 St. Louis, Missouri, Olympics. The first individual Canadian to win an Olympic gold medal for Canada was Montreal policeman Étienne Desmarteau (1873–1905), for the 57-pound hammer throw at the 1904 St. Louis games. In his day, Desmarteau was unbeatable in tug-of-war and other weight sports.

3 Marc Gagnon from Chicoutimi, Quebec, is Canada's most decorated winter Olympian. He has won three Olympic gold and two bronze medals, in Lillehammer, Nagano and Salt Lake. At Salt Lake, Gagnon and Isabelle Charest of Montreal became the first Canadians to win Winter Olympic medals in three consecutive Games.

4 William Sherring (1877–1954), who ran for the St. Patrick's Athletic Club of Hamilton, Ontario. After winning the 1906 Olympic marathon, Sherring received a live goat from the Greeks and a $5,000 award from Hamilton City Council on his triumphant return home.

5 George Hodgson. In addition to winning two gold medals in swimming at the 1912 Stockholm Games, while serving as an officer of the British Royal Naval Air Service during World War I he received medals for his heroic performance in water—this time for rescues made at sea.

6 Pete Desjardins was born in 1907 at St. Pierre, Manitoba, but became an American citizen after moving to Miami Beach. He won gold in the springboard and highboard in 1924 and 1928, when he received a perfect 10 score in two of his three metre dives and an average of 9.2 for 10 dives.

7 The Winnipeg Falcons won gold at the 1920 Antwerp Games, four years before the first games dedicated to winter sports alone. In 1924, at Chamonix, France, Canada's men's hockey team, the Toronto Granites, won the gold medal in what is regarded as the first Winter Olympic games, a gathering of 16 national teams at the International Winter Sports Week.

8 Fanny "Bobbie" Rosenfeld (1905–1969) was voted Canada's Female Athlete of the Half Century in 1950. She took the silver medal in the 100 metres sprint at the 1928 Olympics in Amsterdam, with fellow Canadian Ethel Smith coming in third. Both women were also part of the gold medal win in the 4 x 100-metre relay race, run in world record time.

9 In 1926, Ethel Catherwood, nicknamed the Saskatoon Lily for her beauty and her Saskatchewan roots, broke the world record for the high jump and, at the 1928 Amsterdam Olympics, broke the record again, claiming the first gold medal ever awarded to a female high jumper. She is the only Canadian female athlete to have won an individual gold medal in a track and field

event at the Olympics. Shortly afterward, she married Dr. Harold M. Osborn, winner of the high jump and decathlon gold medals at the 1924 Los Angeles Olympics.

10 Barbara Ann Scott won Canada's first gold medal for figure skating in the 1948 Olympics in St. Moritz.

11 Lucille Wheeler of St-Jovite, Quebec, won the bronze medal in the downhill event at the Cortina Winter Olympics in 1956 which was the first Olympic ski medal awarded to a Canadian. Wheeler started skiing at age 2, won her first national junior ski title at age 12; was named to the Canadian team at age 14, then trained for five winters in Kitzbuhel, Austria, with coach Pepi Salvenmoser. In 1958 she won gold for Canada in both the downhill and the giant slalom titles at the FIS World Championships.

12 Dr. R. Tait McKenzie (1867–1938), formerly an all-around athlete at the Canadian intercollegiate level. His original five-foot diameter medallion in plaster won the art competition at the 1932 Los Angeles Olympics. It contains figures representing every athletic event at the 1932 games.

13 Was she beaten by a man? Well, not quite. Montrealer Hilda Strike, who died in 1989, finished in a dead heat with American-based Polish athlete Stella Walsh in 11.9 seconds, but the judges gave Walsh the medal. In 1980, at age 89, Stella Walsh was killed as an innocent bystander in a robbery in Cleveland. The coroner reported that although Walsh was legally a woman, she had non-functional male sex organs, and most of her chromosomes were male. The IOC did nothing to award Hilda Strike her due. Strike also picked up another silver medal as a member of Canada's 4 x 100-metre relay team.

14 The game's inventor, Dr. James Naismith, from Almonte, Ontario, was there to watch the Canadian team win silver in basketball at the 1936 Berlin Olympics.

15 The Canadian four-man bobsled team, composed of Vic Emery, his brother John, Peter Kirby and Doug Anakin, won the gold. The quartet won in spite of the fact that there were neither training facilities nor tracks in Canada.

16 Nancy Greene won an Olympic gold medal in the giant slalom and a silver in the slalom at the Winter Games in Grenoble, France. She also won two consecutive overall World Cup championships in 1967 and 1968.

17 Harry Jerome (1940–1982) set two world records in sprinting and won a bronze Olympic medal. He died tragically of a heart attack at the age of 42.

18 Karen Magnussen took a silver medal at Sapporo in Japan. Her follow-up victory at the World Figure Skating championship in 1973 was the last by a Canadian female singles skater.

NAC

Karen Magnussen at the 1972 Winter Olympics in Sapporo, Japan.

19 Kathy Kreiner, gold medallist in giant slalom, XIIth Olympic Winter Games, Innsbruck, Austria, was the youngest competitor at the Games four years earlier in Sapporo, Japan.

20 Toller Cranston won a bronze for figure skating.

21 Fellow Crazy Canuck Steve Podborski, who took the bronze medal. Podborski also raced at Sarajevo in 1984, but finished out of the medals.

22 None. Canada retains this dubious record of being the only host country never to win gold at an Olympic Games. What little joy was provided to Canadians at the Montreal games came from Greg Joy, who won the silver medal for his high jump in the rain. In 1978, he went on to break the world record for the high jump with a leap of 2.31 metres.

23 Canada's highest Winter Olympic medal count came at the 2002 Salt Lake City games: six gold, three silver and eight bronze, for a total of 17. Canada's previous best Winter Olympic showing was in Nagano in 1998 with 15 medals and was the first time Canada finished ahead of the United States since the Winter Olympics began in 1924.

24 Elvis Stojko won silver at Lillehammer in 1994 and was awarded the Lionel Conacher Award for Athlete of the Year by the Canadian Press. He accomplished a second Olympic Silver Medal performance at Nagano with a pulled groin muscle. He was the first person to land a quadruple jump combination in a figure-skating competition.

25 Catriona LeMay Doan, in the 500-metre speedskating at Salt Lake City, February 14, 2002, became the first Canadian to defend her individual gold medal after winning the same gold four years earlier in Nagano. Marnie McBean and Kathleen Heddle, as a team, won gold in double sculls at both Barcelona and Atlanta.

26 Myriam Bédard, from Loretteville, Quebec, won gold in the 7.5-and-15 kilometre biathlon events at the 1994 Lillehammer Olympic Games. She took up the biathlon while an army cadet at age 15, using borrowed skis and oversized boots.

27 In 1976, Sue Holloway (1955–) competed in a cross-country skiing race at the Innsbruck games, then paddled as a kayak competitor at Montreal that summer. She was the first Canadian woman ever to compete in both the Winter Olympics and the Summer Olympics in the same year. Holloway finally won medals at the 1984 Olympic Games in Los Angeles, taking a silver and a bronze medal in kayak.

28 Alwyn Morris (1957–) who won a gold and bronze medal with Hugh Fisher in the kayak competition at the 1984 Olympics. On the medal podium he held aloft an eagle feather to honour his Mohawk heritage. A promoter of athletics among First Nations youth, Morris was awarded the 1992 Johnny F. Bassett Memorial Award, given to the Canadian amateur athlete who has displayed a combination of sporting excellence and community values.

29 In the 1984 Summer Olympics at Los Angeles, the Canadians took home a total of 44 medals—10 gold, 18 silver and 16 bronze—the largest number Canada has won at a single Olympic competition. The games had a record attendance of 5.5 million people despite the Soviet-led boycott. Canada's golds included Victor Davis in 200-metre breaststroke; Linda Thom in match pistols; Lori Fung in rhythmic gymnastics; Ann Ottenbrite in 200-metre breaststroke; Sylvie Bernier in springboard diving; and the Men's Eight rowing team.

30 In 1988, Carolyn Waldo, as a solo synchronized swimmer and with partner Michelle Cameron, was Canada's first female athlete to win two gold medals in one Olympics. Waldo also dominated the 1986 World championships, claiming top positions for all events—solo, duet, figures and team. She is currently working as a sportscaster at the local CTV station in Ottawa (CJOH).

31 Silken Laumann (1964–) was named Canada's female athlete of the year in 1991 and again in 1992 after winning bronze at Barcelona with a specially fitted brace for her broken ankle. She won the Lou Marsh award in 1991 as Canada's outstanding athlete; in 1994 she was disqualified at the Pan American Games in Argentina when she tested positive for a drug contained in a cold medication; in 1996 she won the silver medal at Atlanta and retired shortly after.

32 On July 27, 1996, Donovan Bailey won the 100-metre sprint in 9.84 seconds, setting a new world record. At Lake Lanier on the same day, Canadian rowers Marnie McBean and Kathleen Heddle also won gold in the double sculls.

33 After winning two rowing gold medals at Barcelona, Marnie McBean and Kathleen Heddle became Canada's first and only three-time Olympic gold medalists with their victory in Atlanta.

34 Kingston, Ontario, known for its predictable afternoon winds, hosted the yachting events of the 1976 Montreal Olympics.

35 The Soviet invasion of Afghanistan resulted in 80 countries, Canada included, boycotting the 1980 Moscow Summer Olympics.

36 Rowing, with eight golds, is the Summer Olympics sport in which Canada has had the greatest success, followed by seven gold medals in swimming.

37 Alex "Sasha" Baumann set world records in the 200-metre individual medley (2:01.42) and 400-metre individual medley (4:17.41) at the 1984 Summer Olympics in Los Angeles when he won Canada's first swimming gold medals since George Hodgson won two gold medals in swimming at the 1912 Stockholm Games. Born in Prague, Czech Republic, in 1964, he moved with his parents to Canada at age 9 and settled in Sudbury. By age 17 in 1981 he held 51 provincial and 38 national records, and was swimming 14 kilometres daily in training. At age 18 he set a world record in the 200-metre individual medley. Forced out of competition for 10 months with a pulled shoulder, he was back at the Brisbane Commonwealth Games in 1982, where he again won the 200-metre individual medley in world record time. Following the Olympics, Baumann took up coaching in Australia.

38 Victor Davis, born at Guelph, Ontario, in 1964, died on November 28, 1989, in a tragic car accident outside a Montreal bar. A ferocious competitor, Davis got his first world record in the 200-metre breaststroke at the Worlds in Ecuador in 1982. In 1983 he suffered a bout of mononucleosis and then in 1984 he smashed the 200-metre world record at the Los Angeles Olympics, winning gold in a time of 2:13:34, as well as taking home a silver in the 100-metre breaststroke and the 4 x 100-metre medley relay. In 1986 he won the gold medal in the 100-metres at the Commonwealth Games and the World championships. In 1988 he won silver as a member of Canada's 4 x 100-metre medley relay team at the Seoul Olympics.

CANADA GOES CURLING

Curling in Montreal, 1855.

1 How many Canadians curl?
A. Ten thousand
B. Three hundred thousand
C. One million
D. Six million

2 Where was curling invented?
A. Canada
B. Scotland
C. Holland
D. Norway

3 Where were the first curling rocks found?

4 How many rocks are thrown in one end of a curling match by each rink?
A. Ten
B. Four
C. Eight
D. Twelve

Curlers in Halifax in 1867.

5 Who were the first Canadian curlers?

6 Which Canadian city hosted the first curling club in North America?
A. Toronto
B. Montreal
C. Halifax
D. Saint John

7 Where was Canada's first covered curling rink?

8 When and where was the first international bonspiel?
A. Edinburgh
B. Buffalo
C. Glasgow
D. Halifax

An early nineteenth-century curling club.

9 What curler, born at Minnedosa, Manitoba, had his first major win at the Manitoba Bonspiel in 1923 and took 32 more bonspiels, including six grand aggregates in a row from 1942 to 1947 and wrote a curling best-seller?

10 What famous family name is associated with curlers Ernie, Arnold, Garnet and Wes?

11 What curler, known as The Owl, skipped teams that dominated world curling in the late 1960s by winning both the Canadian championships and the world titles in 1966, 1968 and 1969?

12 What curler's rink won 17 straight games in international play, took three out of the four Canadian Men's champion-ships they entered, and won the World Championship and the Air Canada Silver Broom trophy in 1970 and 1971?

13 When did curling become a Winter Olympic sport?

Sandra Schmirler at the first Olympic curling competition.

14 What is the Canadian Women's Curling Championship called?

15 Who is the Canadian women's skip with the most provincial curling titles?
A. Colleen Jones
B. Sandra Schmirler
C. Kelly Law
D. Connie Laliberte

93

1 Some say curling is the most popular sport in Canada. Almost one million Canadians participate in curling, and more than three million TV viewers have tuned in annually for the national championships over the past five years.

2 Most sport historians believe that curling developed in Scotland. The Grand Caledonian Curling Club, later the Royal Caledonian Curling Club, was founded in 1838 at Edinburgh to become Scotland's national governing body and to standardize rules for international play. Within 30 years, a branch of the Royal Caledonian was established in Canada. However, Breughel paintings show a similar game played in Holland in the 1500s, indicating that a kind of curling was invented in Holland.

3 Water-smoothed curling (channel) stones have been found in Scotland dating from 1500. Thumb or stick holes were cut in the top. Modern-day curling rocks are made of rare, dense and polished granite quarried only on Ailsa Craig, an island off Scotland's coast. Each rock weighs 42 pounds. The sport is called "curling" because the stones rotate when they are released and follow a curved path to the target.

4 Eight rocks are thrown in each end of a curling match, two each by the four members of the rink—the lead, second, third (or vice skip) and skip.

5 The first curlers in Canada were the men of the 78th Highland regiment who played on the St. Charles River in Quebec in 1760. According to W.H. Murray, in *The Curling Companion*, "When they could find no suitable stones they were allowed to melt down cannon balls." The "earliest reports in the Canadian Press are for 1805 at Beauport, near Quebec, and in the town itself at an artificial rink made in 1808 on one of the wharves—the river ice being too rough."

6 A group of Scots formed the Montreal Curling Club, the first curling club in North America, in 1807, followed by clubs in Kingston (1820), Quebec City (1821) and Halifax (1824). According to W.H. Murray, "Quebec Province had no good stones, so they used irons of 45 to 65 pounds—at first roughly shaped with high sides."

7 On December 15, 1869, Prince Arthur opened the Montreal Curling Club, the city's first covered curling rink.

8 A Canadian curling rink first toured Scotland in 1908 where they won 23 of 26 matches, but the first international bonspiel took place in 1835, in Buffalo, New York, between US and Canadian clubs.

9 Ken Watson (1904–1986) was born at Minnedosa, Manitoba. His career Macdonald Briar record is 25 and 2 and, in 1949, he and his Strathcona Manitoba rink were the first to win the Tankard three times. He also wrote the best-seller *Ken Watson on Curling*.

10 The Richardsons, Ernie, Arnold, Garnet, and Wes, won four Canadian and world curling championships between 1959 and 1963.

11 Ron Northcott (1935–) born at Innisfail, Alberta, was known as The Owl. He started curling at age 15 in Vulcan, Alberta, and was vice-skip on the 1953 Alberta High School champions. In 1958 he joined the Calgary Curling Club and from 1961 to 1978 he competed in nine Alberta championships. He represented Alberta at six Canadian Briers.

12 Don Duguid (1935–) and his rink won 17 straight games in international play. After retiring, Duguid covered the world championship for CBC-TV and started several curling schools.

13 Curling first became an Olympic sport at the Nagano Winter Olympics in 1998, where the winners were Canada's women's team skipped by Sandra Schmirler and Switzerland's men's team. Curling had been a demonstration Olympic sport four times—in 1924 (Chamonix, France), 1932 (Lake Placid, NY), 1988 (Calgary) and 1992 (Albertville, France). At the Calgary Games in 1988, curling was a demonstration sport, but the 21,000 tickets for six days of competition sold out faster than every sport except figure skating and speedskating.

14 The Scott Tournament of Hearts is the current Canadian Women's Curling Championship. It was established in 1982. The Canadian Men's championship is called The Briar. The World Curling Championship is called the Air Canada Silver Broom and was established in 1968. Canadians won the first five competitions.

15 Colleen Jones from Nova Scotia has won her provincial title 13 times, as well as the Tournament of Hearts in 1982, 1999, 2000 and 2002. In 2002, Jones became the first woman to win four titles as a skip.

1 Where and when was the first recorded game of baseball?

2 Who was the first Canadian-born major leaguer?

3 Name the Canadian who invented the baseball glove.

4 Where did Babe Ruth hit his first home run?

5 In 1947, Jackie Robinson broke the racial barrier and became the first black baseball player in the major leagues. What team did he play for in the Brooklyn Dodgers minor league system?

Canadian Baseball Hall-of-Famer in action against the Montreal Expos in 1970.

6 Who is the only Canadian elected to the Baseball Hall of Fame?

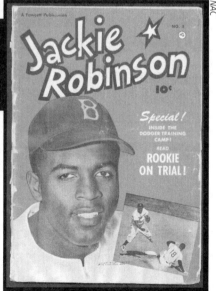

The cover of a 1951 Jackie Robinson paperback.

7 Name the trophy that the Blue Jays and Expos play for once each year during the regular season.

8 Name the financially disastrous weekly baseball betting pool begun to raise funds to finance Ottawa's share of the 1988 Winter Olympic Games.

9 Name the first player of a Canadian-based team to win baseball's Most Valuable Player Award.

10 Where is the home of the Canadian Baseball Hall of Fame and Museum?

11 Name the Expo manager who led the team to its first playoff appearance.

12 On April 8, 1969, the National Baseball League's Montreal Expos played their first game. Where was the stadium, who threw out the first pitch, and who did they play?

13 What Expo player was given the nickname "Hawk"?

14 On April 13, 1984, Montreal fans welcomed a new player in his first game as an Expo. He promptly hit a double, his 4,000th career hit. Who was he?

15 What Expo player was given the nickname "Scoop"?

16 Who pitched the Expos' first two no-hitters?

17 Name the first Canadian-born pitcher to play for the Expos.

18 In what year did major league baseball players go on strike and the Expos make the playoffs?

19 Name the Expo pitcher known as the "Spaceman."

20 Where were people when they sat in "Jonesville"?

21 Which team did the Toronto Blue Jays play in their first regular season game on April 7, 1977, and what was noteworthy about the game?

22 Why was the Jays' 1987 season such a bummer?

23 Which team did the Blue Jays play in their first game in the SkyDome?

24 What was noteworthy about the first Jays win at the SkyDome?

25 In 1991, the Minnesota Twins beat the Blue Jays 8–5 at the SkyDome to win the American League pennant; what was noteworthy about this game for Blue Jays manager Cito Gaston?

26 What baseball shortstop, born at St. Paul, Minnesota, signed as free agent with the Toronto Blue Jays on December 7, 1992, after 15 years with the Milwaukee Brewers?

27 On October 18, 1992, in Atlanta, Georgia, the visiting Toronto Blue Jays beat the Atlanta Braves 5–4 in game two of the World Series to tie the series at one game apiece. What happened in the pre-game ceremony to mar the festivities? And what was remarkable about the game?

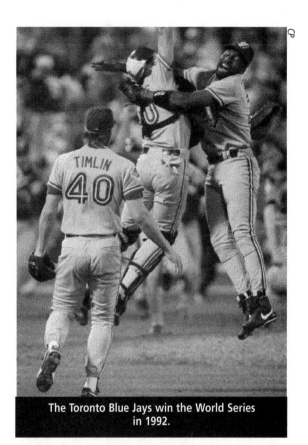

The Toronto Blue Jays win the World Series in 1992.

28 In 1993, the Blue Jays became the first team in American League history to have teammates finish 1-2-3 in the batting race. Name the players.

29 Why was the October 20, 1993, Jays vs. Phillies match called "the ugliest game in World Series history"?

30 Name the player who left the Blue Jays to play basketball for the Boston Celtics.

1 The first recorded baseball game was played on June 4, 1838, in Beachville, Ontario, about 40 kilometres east of London, Ontario. This game took place a year before Abner Doubleday supposedly "invented" the game in Cooperstown, New York. The source of this claim is a letter published in the Philadelphia *Sporting Life* magazine of May 5, 1886, entitled "A Game of Long-ago Which Closely Resembled Our Present National Game." The writer was Dr. Adam Ford of Denver, Colorado, who had grown up in Beachville. Ford's letter has a diagram of a five-sided playing field, showing where the balls were "fair hit" or "no hit" (foul). The number of men on each side, usually between 7 and 12 players per team, had to be equal before a game could be played.

2 Bill Phillips, a first baseman from Saint John, New Brunswick, who signed with Cleveland in 1879, was the first Canadian to play in the National League.

3 Toronto shortstop Arthur "Foxy" Irwin. In 1883, after breaking two fingers on his left hand while playing for the National League's Providence Grays, he adapted an oversized buckskin driving glove by padding it, making a fastening at the back and leaving room for his bandages. Soon most professional players were wearing what was called the "Irwin glove." Irwin went on to become a successful major league manager.

4 On September 5, 1914, playing for the Providence Grays against the Maple Leafs in the Toronto Island stadium. In the sixth inning, 19-year-old Ruth hit his first professional home run off Toronto pitcher Ellis Johnson. Ruth also pitched his best game of the season, beating the Leafs 9–0. In 1985 a plaque was unveiled at Hanlan's Point where the baseball stadium once stood.

5 The Montreal Royals were the Triple-A level International League minor league affiliate of the Brooklyn Dodgers. In 1945, Dodger manager Branch Rickey signed Robinson and black pitcher John Wright to play for the Royals. He felt able to sign an African-American player before any other owner in part because Montreal was considered to be the most cosmopolitan city in North America. On April 18, 1946, at Jersey City, Robinson had his first four hits, including a three-run homer, as the Royals beat Jersey 14–1. Robinson played for the Royals for a year and topped the league with a .349 average, leading the Royals to the International League pennant and a spot in the Little World Series against Louisville. Rickey moved him up to the Dodgers in 1947, saying, "I'm looking for a ballplayer with guts enough not to fight back." Robinson was the first black American elected to baseball's Hall of Fame.

6 Pitcher Ferguson Jenkins is the only Canadian in the Baseball Hall of Fame, elected in 1991. He hails from Chatham, Ontario. Fergie Jenkins had a pro career of 19 seasons with the Chicago Cubs as one of the top pitchers in the major leagues during the 1960s and 1970s, winning 284 games and striking out 3,192 batters.

7 The Pearson Cup game was first played on June 29, 1978. This annual competition between the Toronto Blue Jays and the Montreal Expos is named for the former prime minister, who was an avid baseball player and fan. Proceeds from this exhibition game go to support amateur baseball in Canada.

8 Sport Select Baseball was begun and halted in 1984. The baseball betting pool, intended to help finance Ottawa's share of the 1988 Winter Olympic Games, was doomed

after meeting opposition from the provinces and major league baseball, because they saw the scheme as an invasion of their territory.

9 Toronto Blue Jay George Bell won baseball's MVP Award in 1987. In 1993 the Jays' Paul Molitor (replacing Dave Winfield) was named Series MVP, with an even .500 with eight runs batted in.

10 St. Marys, Ontario, was selected to be the site of the Canadian Baseball Hall of Fame on August 25, 1994. A 30-acre site adjacent to the St. Marys quarry houses an old stadium and museum with artifacts of Canadian baseball history. According to University of Western Ontario professor Bob Barney, Adam Ford, an early mayor of St. Marys, chronicled Canada's first game at nearby Beachville in 1838.

11 Dick Williams led the Expos to their first playoffs. Charlie Finley hired him away after one year to manage the Oakland A's.

12 Lester B. Pearson threw out the first ball at Jarry Park for the Montreal Expos' first game on April 8, 1969. The Expos beat their first opponents, the St. Louis Cardinals, 8–7 in the first regular-season major league baseball game in Canada, and the first outside the USA.

13 Andre Dawson was nicknamed "Hawk."

14 Pete Rose scored this record hit as a Montreal Expo against his former teammates, the Philadelphia Phillies, and became the only National League player to reach 4,000 career hits since Ty Cobb got 4,109 total hits with American League teams Detroit and Philadelphia.

15 "Scoop" was Al Oliver's nickname.

16 On April 17, 1969, the two-week-old Expos recorded their first no-hitter, as Bill

Stoneman blanked the Phillies 7–0 at Philadelphia. On October 2, 1972, Bill Stoneman pitched his second career no-hitter, a 7–0 win over the Mets at Jarry Park.

17 Claude Raymond was the Expos' first Canadian-born pitcher.

18 In 1981 the Expos made it to the National League playoffs, but on Blue Monday, October 19, 1981, Dodgers outfielder Rick Monday blasted a game-winning, ninth-inning home run off Steve Rogers in the fifth and deciding game of the National League Championship Series at Olympic Stadium. The Dodgers took the championship three games to two and went on to beat the Yankees in the Fall Classic. For the third consecutive season, the Expos were eliminated by the eventual World Series winners.

19 Bill Lee was the "Spaceman."

20 "Jonesville" was a section of Jarry Park, way out in left field.

21 In a light snowfall at the CNE Exhibition Stadium, the expansion Jays beat the Chicago White Sox 9–5. Al Woods, pinch-hitting for Steve Bowling in the fifth inning, hit a home run in his first at bat. It was the first American League baseball game played outside the United States.

22 On October 4, 1987, the Detroit Tigers beat the second-place Jays 1–0 at Tiger Stadium on Larry Herndon's second-inning home run, to win the AL East title; they were one game behind the Jays entering their three-game season-ending showdown, and won each game by a single run (4–3, 3–2, and 1–0); the Blue Jays lost their final seven games, allowing the Tigers to beat them in the division on the last day of the regular season.

23 On June 5, 1989, the Jays lost 5–3 to the Milwaukee Brewers in their first game in the SkyDome. The first pitch by Jimmy Key to Paul Molitor was a curve-ball strike; that ball now rests in the Baseball Hall of Fame. The Blue Jays' first victory in the SkyDome came on June 7, 1989. Ernie Whitt had three hits and drove in three runs as the Toronto Blue Jays beat the Milwaukee Brewers 4–2 before over 45,000 fans.

24 The Blue Jays' first win at the SkyDome was the first game in major league history played indoors and outdoors on the same day. With rain threatening in the fifth inning, the operators started closing the $100 million retractable roof at 8:48 p.m., finishing 34 minutes later, but too late to prevent a short game delay.

25 Cito Gaston was the first manager ever ejected in a baseball playoff game.

26 Paul Molitor, who led the Jays to their second straight World Series title as the series MVP, joined the team as a free agent in December 1992. He batted .418 in two World Series appearances (1982, 1993) and was the only player to hit five for five in a World Series. He holds the designated hitter record for stolen bases (24).

27 A US Marine Corps colour guard entered the stadium mistakenly carrying the Canadian flag upside down. With their victory the Jays became the first non-American team to win a World Series game. Six days later Dave Winfield whacked a two-run double in the 11th inning to give the Toronto Blue Jays a 4–3 win over Atlanta, and baseball's World Series, four games to two. They became the first team from outside the United States to take the World Series title.

28 John Olerud led the American League in 1993 with a .363 batting average, followed by fellow Blue Jays Paul Molitor at .332 and Roberto Alomar at .326; this was the first time the top three hitters came from the same team.

29 The October 20, 1993, match between Toronto and Philadelphia was the highest scoring game in World Series and post-season history, with the most runs scored by both teams. It was also the longest ever World Series game, at four hours, 14 minutes. The Jays beat Mitch Williams and the Phillies relief corps, scoring six runs in the eighth inning to overcome a 14–9 deficit; Toronto reliever Duane Ward retired all four batters he faced in Toronto's 15–14 win.

30 Danny Ange left the Jays to play basketball for the Celts.

Geography?

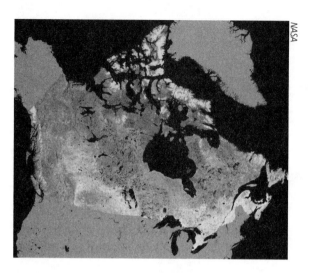

NASA

1 How does Canada rank among the largest countries of the world by area?
A. First
B. Second
C. Third
D. Fourth

2 What important historical event occurred at Batoche National Historic Site located near Saskatoon, Saskatchewan?

3 What town served as the basis for the fictional town of Mariposa in Stephen Leacock's *Sunshine Sketches of a Little Town*?

4 Kensington Market is in the heart of downtown Toronto. What is the name of the outdoor market in downtown Ottawa?

5 In which city would you find Cavendish Square?

6 Which city is known as "Hogtown"?

7 On what street in Ottawa do you find the Parliament Buildings?

8 "Depot Division" is found in what western Canadian city?

9 What old Ottawa hotel is beside Parliament Hill and the Rideau Canal?

An early aerial view of Ottawa.

Library of Congress

10 The ghost of this Upper Canada rebel is said to haunt a house at 82 Bond Street in Toronto.

11 In which two provinces can you find Utopia?

12 Name the northern Saskatchewan mining town that calls itself a city and nearly became a ghost town when Eldorado Nuclear closed its operations in 1981.

13 In what city was Sir John A. Macdonald buried?

14 Both Ontario and New Brunswick have cities named Chatham; what two provinces both have towns named Woodstock?

15 In which province can you find the town of Moscow?

16 What is the name of the westernmost community in Canada?
A. Beaver Creek
B. Port Hardy
C. Cape Spear
D. Queen Charlotte's Landing

17 What is the most southerly city in Canada?
A. Victoria, BC
B. Niagara Falls, ON
C. Windsor, ON

20 The world's longest undefended international border is the 49th parallel. Name Canada's provincial capitals that lie north of the 49th parallel.

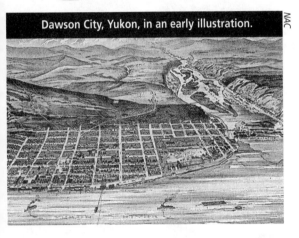

Dawson City, Yukon, in an early illustration.

NAC

18 What Canadian city had a population of more than 25,000 in the late 1800s, but has only 700 residents today?
A. Louisbourg, NS
B. Barkerville, BC
C. Dawson City, Yukon

19 What is the world's most northerly permanent settlement?

21 Because of the islands of St. Pierre and Miquelon, France is one of the four countries closest to Canada, along with the USA and Russia. What is the fourth country?

22 Which of these provinces extends the farthest south?
A. British Columbia
B. Newfoundland
C. Nova Scotia

23 Name the three provinces that have borders with only one other province.

24 How did mapmakers settle the original dispute between New Brunswick and Quebec over possession of Madawaska County?

25 Which two provinces have the shortest border between them?

26 Which province has no skunks, poison ivy or snakes?

27 How many provinces do not have salt water coastlines?

28 This promontory in Newfoundland is the most easterly point of Canada.

29 Why are Nova Scotians called Bluenosers?

30 Île Bizard, Île des Soeurs and Île Perrot are parts of this metropolitan area.

31 What river was used to define the border between Upper and Lower Canada?

32 In what city was Terry Fox forced to end his Marathon of Hope cross-country run in 1980?

33 What Nova Scotia Island may be the burial place for Captain Kidd's pirate treasure?
A. Sable Island
B. Lennox Island
C. Magdalen Island
D. Oak Island

34 What is special about St. Peter's Church in Windermere, British Columbia?

35 Where is the only walled city in North America?

NAC

36 Where is the only post office in the world that bears the name of beloved Austrian composer Wolfgang Amadeus Mozart?

37 Where in Nova Scotia will you find the country's only post office in a lighthouse?

Tourism NS

38 What is the nickname for the tourist attraction in Moncton, New Brunswick, where, due to an optical illusion, cars appear to roll uphill?

39 The Golden Boy statue on top of the Manitoba Legislature in Winnipeg almost never made it to Manitoba. Why?

40 Two Canadian cities have hosted world's fairs. Where and when were they held?

41 The International Peace Garden is on the border between what Canadian province and American state?

42 Yellowknife is on the shore of what lake?

43 Where can you find the largest French Canadian community on the Prairies?

44 What body of water separates Newfoundland from Labrador?

45 Where is the town of Moose Factory located?

46 What town is home to a giant *Tyrannosaurus rex*?

47 What Canadian city straddles a provincial border and has two provincial premiers?

48 What capital city has a Royal Canadian Mint that is the only one producing circulating coinage for Canada?

49 Where did Dutch Queen Juliana give birth to her eldest daughter?

50 A statue of a giant Canada goose is a landmark in which Canadian town?
A. Vulcan, Alberta
B. Steinbach, Manitoba
C. Wawa, Ontario
D. Outlook, Saskatchewan

51 Wayne Gretzky was born and started scoring goals in what Ontario town?

52 Name three eastern Canadian capital cities located on islands.

53 First inhabited mostly by American lumbermen, this city was once known as Wrightstown and is sometimes referred to as Ottawa's twin city.

54 Voters in Winnipeg were the first in a major Canadian city to elect an openly gay mayor. Who was he?
A. Michael Phair
B. Glen Murray
C. Peter Kaufmann
D. James Richardson

55 Sir Henry Pellatt built the Casa Loma castle in Toronto. Where is Craigdarroch Castle built by coal magnate James Dunsmuir located?
A. Halifax
B. Windsor
C. Victoria
D. Hamilton

56 Which city does not rank as one of Canada's top-10 cities by population?
A. Hamilton, Ontario
B. London, Ontario
C. Halifax, Nova Scotia
D. Winnipeg, Manitoba

57 Which two northern capitals both have a colour in their names?

58 A monument to Wolfe and Montcalm stands outside the Chateau Frontenac in Quebec City. One of the oldest monuments in Montreal, however, is of this British admiral.

59 The sculpture in Nathan Phillips Square in front of Toronto's City Hall is called "The Archer." Who was the artist?

60 What is the meaning of Newfoundland's motto, *Quaerite Prime Regnum Dei*?

61 What are the ingredients in a Newfoundland pie?

62 What province is known for Double Daylight Savings Time?

63 What was the original name proposed for British Columbia?
A. New Westminster
B. New Britain
C. New Caledonia

64 Which province has the largest share of its population living on farms?
A. Alberta
B. Saskatchewan
C. Manitoba
D. Quebec

65 Which province has an official holiday called Family Day?

66 Does any province touch more than two other provinces?

67 What province is the leading producer of maple syrup?

68 What was the last province to join Confederation?

69 In the Prairie Provinces, French is not the second largest population by mother tongue. What language is?

70 Which province has the lowest telephone area code number?

1 Canada is the second largest country in the world by area, after Russia, which includes the vast region of Siberia. Canada contains 9,970,610 square kilometres, reaching from the Atlantic to the Pacific and Arctic Oceans. Russia is the world's largest nation, with an area of 17,075,040 square kilometres. Canada occupies seven of the world's twenty-four time zones; Russia occupies nine.

2 The Batoche National Historic Site was the location of the Northwest Rebellion, where the combined forces of Louis Riel and Gabriel Dumont were defeated on May 12, 1885.

3 Orillia, Ontario, is the original for Stephen Leacock's fictional town of Mariposa. Parks Canada operates the Leacock home at Brewery Bay as a museum.

4 Byward Market is in downtown Ottawa.

5 Cavendish Square is in the city of St. John's, Newfoundland.

6 "Hogtown" was one of the nicknames for Toronto because of its meat-packing industries.

7 The Parliament Buildings are on Wellington Street in Ottawa.

8 "Depot Division" is the moniker for the RCMP Training Centre in Regina.

9 The Chateau Laurier is the grand hotel in Ottawa beside Parliament Hill and the Rideau Canal.

10 The ghost of William Lyon Mackenzie is said to haunt 82 Bond Street in Toronto.

11 Utopia is a town in both Manitoba and Ontario.

12 Uranium City, Saskatchewan, nearly became a ghost town when Eldorado Nuclear pulled out in 1981.

13 Sir John A. Macdonald was buried in Kingston, Ontario.

14 In addition to sharing cities named Chatham, Ontario and New Brunswick also share towns named Woodstock. Towns with this name can be found near London, Ontario, and near Fredericton, New Brunswick.

15 Moscow is a town in Ontario.

16 Beaver Creek, Yukon, just a few kilometres east of the Alaska border, is Canada's westernmost community.

17 The most southerly city in Canada is Windsor, Ontario.

18 Dawson City had almost 30,000 residents in the 1800s because of the Klondike gold rush, and was the largest community north of Seattle and west of Winnipeg. Today its population is 700. Dawson was named after George Mercer Dawson (1849–1901), explorer, scientist and director of the Geological and Natural History Survey of Canada from 1895 to 1901. A son of geologist Sir John Dawson, G.M. Dawson suffered from a severe illness at age 12, leaving him hunchbacked and crippled for the rest of his life. But after graduating from the Royal School of Mines in London, England, at the top of his class, he carried out some of the most strenuous surveys ever attempted in Canada.

19 The weather station at Alert, Northwest Territories, is the world's most northerly settlement, located at the northern end of Ellesmere Island in Canada's North. Canada's most northern point is Cape Columbia, Nunavut, at latitude 83°7' north.

20 Edmonton, Regina and Winnipeg are the only provincial capitals north of the 49th parallel.

21 Greenland is an autonomous province of Denmark, making Denmark one of Canada's four closest neighbours.

22 Nova Scotia extends the farthest south by land of these three provinces. However, Middle Island, Ontario, in Lake Erie, is Canada's southernmost piece of territory, at latitude 41°41' north. Twenty-seven of the 50 US states have land north of Middle Island.

23 Newfoundland, Nova Scotia and British Columbia are the three provinces that border only one other province.

24 The possession of Madawaska County was settled between New Brunswick and Quebec by a roll of the dice.

25 New Brunswick and Nova Scotia share the shortest border between two provinces.

26 Newfoundland.

27 Only two provinces do not have salt water coastlines, Alberta and Saskatchewan.

28 Cape Spear, Newfoundland, is the most easterly point of Canada.

29 Nova Scotians may be called Bluenosers because of their fondness for Irish Bluenose potatoes, or the nickname may come from a derisory epithet given to them by Bostonians, who noted the marks that were left on the noses of Nova Scotian fishermen by their blue mittens.

30 Île Bizard, Île des Soeurs and Île Perrot are all in Montreal.

31 The Ottawa River defined the border between Upper and Lower Canada.

32 Thunder Bay, Ontario, is where Terry Fox was forced to end his Marathon of Hope run across Canada, when it was determined that cancer had spread to his lungs. His running resulted in $623 million in contributions to the National Cancer Institute of Canada.

33 Oak Island in Nova Scotia may be the secret burial place for Captain Kidd's pirate treasure. Six fortune seekers have died looking for his treasure around a booby-trapped well.

34 St. Peter's Church in Windermere, BC, is stolen property. When the CPR moved its local headquarters from Donald to Revelstoke in 1897, thus sentencing the town of Donald to death, the local people asked that their Anglican church be moved to Windermere. The CPR said no, so the parishioners dismantled it and moved it piece by piece over rails and river ferries to its new home, 185 kilometres south of Donald. The bell didn't make it, having been stolen en route by another group of churchgoers from the nearby village of Golden.

35 Quebec City is the only walled city in North America and the first to be placed on the United Nations Educational, Scientific, and Cultural Organization's (UNESCO's) World Heritage list. Quebec was awarded World Heritage status, which designates the city as belonging to all humanity and to be preserved as such, on July 3, 1986, as part of a week-long celebration.

36 Mozart, Saskatchewan, is the only city in the world so named.

37 The lighthouse at picturesque Peggy's Cove, Nova Scotia, perched on its base of wave-worn granite, no longer serves as a beacon but is still used as the village's post office.

38 At Magnetic Hill, New Brunswick, an optical illusion in the landscape makes cars appear to roll uphill.

39 The Golden Boy statue in Winnipeg was sculpted by Georges Gardet, then cast in bronze by a foundry outside Paris in 1918, the final year of World War I. But when the foundry was partially destroyed in a German bombing raid, the statue was temporarily lost. Finally found intact in its packing case, the Golden Boy was shipped to Manitoba and placed on top of the Legislative Building in Winnipeg on November 21, 1919. The Golden Boy was gilded in 1951, and his torch lit on December 31, 1966, to mark Canada's centennial.

The site of Expo 67 in Montreal.

40 Montreal hosted over 50 million visitors at the World's Fair Expo 67. Vancouver hosted over 20 million visitors at Expo 86.

41 Established in 1932, the International Peace Garden spans the Canada–US border at Boissevain, Manitoba, and Dunseith, North Dakota.

42 Yellowknife is on the shore of Great Slave Lake.

43 St. Boniface, Manitoba, is the largest French Canadian community on the Canadian Prairies, and most of the 47,665 Franco-Manitobans who have French as their mother tongue live there.

44 Newfoundland and Labrador are separated by the Strait of Belle Isle.

45 Moose Factory is in northern Ontario on the shore of James Bay.

46 Dini, a dinosaur made of concrete and standing taller than 10 metres, is found in Drumheller, Alberta. Drumheller is world renowned for the quality of its dinosaur fossiis and its magnificent Tyrell Museum of Paleontology.

47 Lloydminster is situated on the Saskatchewan–Alberta border 300 kilometres west of Prince Albert and 235 kilometres east of Edmonton. Originally called Britannia Settlement, the town found itself neatly sliced in half when Alberta and Saskatchewan were created in 1905. In 1930, the Alberta village of Lloydminster and the Saskatchewan town of the same name amalgamated as the town of Lloydminster by order-in-council in both governments. In 1958 the town was raised to city status.

48 The Royal Canadian Mint in Winnipeg is now the only one producing circulating coinage for Canada.

49 Queen Juliana of Holland lived in exile in Ottawa during World War II and gave birth to her eldest daughter there.

50 Wawa, Ontario, has as its landmark a statue of a giant Canada goose. The name Wawa means "goose" in Ojibway.

51 Wayne Gretzky was born in Brantford, Ontario, in 1961.

52 Charlottetown, Prince Edward Island; St. John's, Newfoundland; and Iqaluit, Nunavut, are all eastern Canadian capital cities located on islands.

53 Hull, Quebec, now part of Gatineau, an amalgam of five municipalities, is Ottawa's twin city.

54 Glen Murray of Winnipeg is Canada's first openly gay mayor.

55 Craigdarroch Castle, built in 1887–90 by Vancouver Island coal magnate James Dunsmuir, is in the Rockland area of Victoria, BC. There is a story that Dunsmuir promised his wife, Joan, that if she would leave Scotland and join him in British Columbia he would build her a castle.

56 Halifax, Nova Scotia, is not one of Canada's largest 10 cities (pre-amalgamation).

57 Whitehorse and Yellowknife are the two "colourful" northern capitals.

58 The statue of Admiral Nelson is one of the oldest monuments in Montreal.

59 "The Archer," in front of Toronto's City Hall, was sculpted by Henry Moore.

60 Newfoundland's Latin motto means "Seek ye first the Kingdom of God."

61 The ingredients in a Newfoundland pie are molasses, eggs and soft bread crumbs.

62 Double Daylight Savings Time occurs in Newfoundland.

63 The original name proposed for the province of British Columbia was New Caledonia.

64 Saskatchewan has the largest percentage of its population living on farms and produces twice as much wheat as all nine others combined.

65 Alberta recognizes Family Day on February 1 as an official holiday and first celebrated it in 1989. In Newfoundland, St. Patrick's Day is taken as an official holiday every March 17, and in British Columbia August 7 is British Columbia Day.

66 Only Quebec touches three other provinces: Ontario to the west, New Brunswick and Newfoundland (Labrador) to the east.

67 Quebec produces more maple syrup than all the other provinces combined. Canada is the world's leading producer of maple syrup.

68 Newfoundland, which joined in 1949, was the last province to enter Confederation.

69 After English, the next most common mother tongue spoken in the Prairie Provinces is German. In British Columbia, the second largest population by mother tongue is Chinese.

70 Manitoba has the lowest area code in Canada—204.

CANADA PLACE NAMES

1 When French explorer Jacques Cartier asked the Iroquois First Nations what their land was called, and pointed to what is now Quebec City, they used the word "kanata." The French took this to be the name for the whole area and, over time, for the entire country. What does the name Canada mean in Iroquois?

2 In 1866, many newspaper editors and citizens came up with their own suggestions for the name of the new country. Name the one that was not suggested as a name for what is now Canada.
A. Britannia
B. Cabotia
C. Canadia
D. Columbia
E. Laurentia
F. New Britain
G. Queensland
H. Ursalia

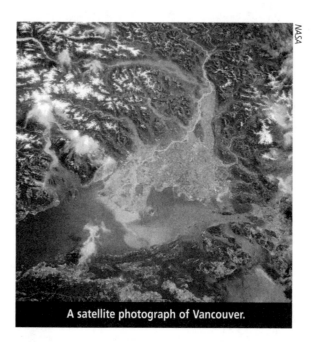

A satellite photograph of Vancouver.

3 Vancouver is named after the navigator Captain George Vancouver, who in 1792 named and explored Burrard Inlet and began a detailed two-and-a-half-year survey of the British Columbia coast. What other famous captain did Vancouver previously sail with?

4 Kelowna was originally named Kimach Touche ("black bear's face"), the Indian name for a hairy hermit named August Gillard who lived in a half-underground den on the townsite. Where does its current name come from?

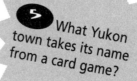

5 What Yukon town takes its name from a card game?

6 Saskatchewan's name comes from the Plains Cree word "kisiskatchewan," meaning "the river that flows swiftly." What is the Cree origin of the name Manitoba?

7 Iqaluit was chosen as the capital of Nunavut, Canada's newest territory. What was the previous name of this community, and what's the origin of the name?

8 Kitchener is a city in southwestern Ontario. What was its original name and why was the name changed?

9 What Ontario town is named after a type of plaster?

10 Who was the town of Florenceville, New Brunswick, named after?

Colonists at Saskatoon in 1903.

14 What Canadian city is named after Queen Victoria's husband?

Satellite photograph of royal Canadian city.

11 Head-Smashed-In Buffalo Jump, 18 kilometres west of Fort Macleod, Alberta, is the world's oldest, largest and best-preserved buffalo jump, and was designated a UNESCO World Heritage Site in 1981. First Nations people used the site for more than 5,500 years, panicking herds of buffalo to stampede along a path that ended at a cliff, where they were killed as a result of falling. What is the origin of the name?

13 The original townsite of Saskatoon, on the east bank of the South Saskatchewan River 235 kilometres northwest of Regina, was part of a 100,000-acre grant in 1882 to the Temperance Colonisation Society of Toronto. The same year, John N. Lake, the leader of that new temperance colony, christened the spot Saskatoon. What did he name Saskatoon after?

15 In July of 2000, Prince Edward, the Earl of Wessex, visited Prince Edward Island. Of course this province is not named after the Queen's youngest child. Who is it named after?
A. The son of King Edward VIII
B. The son of Queen Elizabeth I
C. The son of Queen Victoria
D. The son of King George III

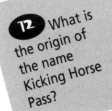
12 What is the origin of the name Kicking Horse Pass?

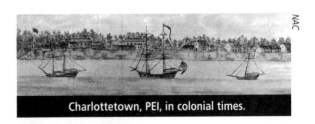
Charlottetown, PEI, in colonial times.

111

The consort of George III with her children, c.1765.

Royal Collection, Windsor

A satellite photograph of Winnipeg.

NASA

16 What provincial capital, incorporated as a town in 1855 and as a city in 1875, is named after the consort of King George III?

17 Who was the province of Alberta named after?
A. Oblate Father Albert Lacombe
B. Queen Victoria's husband, Prince Albert
C. Queen Victoria's daughter Alberta

18 What two Canadian capitals are named after Queen Victoria?

19 This royal Quebec city is famous for the hockey sticks manufactured there.

20 What is the origin of the name Ontario?

21 What was the original name for the city of Toronto?

22 What is the First Nations origin of the name Winnipeg?

23 What is the origin of the name Yellowknife?

NAC

The early settlement on the present location of Toronto.

24 What is the origin of the name Whitehorse?

25 Lachine, Quebec, now part of Montreal, was founded on land granted to fur trader René-Robert Cavelier de La Salle, discoverer of the Mississippi Delta. Why was it called Lachine?

26 In 1784, Cape Breton became a separate colony from mainland Nova Scotia, and lieutenant-governor J.F.W. DesBarres founded a new capital for the colony, naming it after a British viscount who also has an Australian city named after him. What is the name of this Cape Breton town?

27 From 1783 to 1784, over 18,000 Loyalists arrived at the mouth of the Saint John River in New Brunswick and built settlements called Parr Town and Carleton. In 1785 the two settlements took the name of Saint John, from the river, and the new city was granted a royal charter on May 17, 1786, making it the first incorporated city in Canada. What is the origin of the name Saint John?

28 Most accounts say the Hudson's Bay Company trading post Brandon House was named in honour of the Duke of Brandon, an ancestor of Lord Selkirk. Another version of the origin of the name says that a young Scottish aristocrat, Lord Brandon, became romantically involved with an officer's wife from Portage la Prairie, and the irate husband forced him to flee for his life. He lived the rest of his days as a hermit in the hills near the Little Souris and Assiniboine rivers, which became known as the Brandon Hills. What city is at the site of the original trading post?

The first photograph taken in Calgary, 1878.

29 What is the origin of the name of Moose Jaw, in Saskatchewan?

30 In 1905, the Canadian Northern Railway reached a point across the North Saskatchewan River from the county town of Battleford. When the Post Office named the new settlement, citizens of both towns protested. What is the name of this Saskatchewan town?

31 Calgary, Alberta, is named after a Scottish ancestral estate. What does Calgary mean in Gaelic?

1 Most accounts say "*kanata*" means "a meeting place" or "a collection of houses," but some modern Iroquois use the term to mean a settlement, and then add an adjective: for example, the Iroquois village of Kahnawake–Kanata Wake. Some Iroquois still call New York City Kanata, although it should be Kanata Kowa, Big Village.

2 Queensland was *not* one of the many names suggested for Canada.

3 Born in Norfolk in 1757, Vancouver joined the navy at age 14, and sailed with Captain Cook on his second and last voyages of exploration.

4 Kelowna comes from the Okanagan Indian word meaning "female grizzly bear." The name was changed to Kelowna because the original name seemed too uncouth.

5 Faro, Yukon, was named after the card game of the same name, and for the first stakes claimed on the ore body that became the Anvil Mine. Built to house the people from the open-pit lead, zinc and silver mine, the town was destroyed in a forest fire on June 13, 1969, but rebuilt in three months.

6 Manitoba is a Cree term for "The Great Spirit speaks," after a cave in Lake Manitoba which makes sounds when the wind is blowing.

7 Iqaluit was previously named Frobisher Bay. In 1949, the Hudson's Bay Company moved its post to the head of Frobisher Bay, and a town was established that became a municipality in 1971. In December 1984 the residents voted 310–213 to rename the place Iqaluit, an Inuktitut name meaning "place of fish."

8 Kitchener was originally called Berlin. Its name was changed during World War I for patriotic reasons, and to honour Lord Herbert Kitchener, Commandant of the British Army.

9 Paris. The town's 1829 founder, an American named Hiram Capron, named it after the fine clay or gypsum deposits nearby that were used to make plaster of Paris. Situated on the Grand River, the town of Paris was incorporated on March 5, 1838. Long-time residents are called Parisians, others known as Paris-ites.

10 Florenceville, New Brunswick, was named after the famous nurse Florence Nightingale.

11 Head-Smashed-In Buffalo Jump gets its name from one foolhardy brave who wanted to see the buffalo falling from under the shelter of a ledge below the cliff. But the pile of dead buffalo reached higher than expected, and he was found dead, with his head crushed against the cliff by the weight of the buffalo.

12 On August 29, 1858, Dr. James Hector, geologist with the Palliser Expedition, was knocked unconscious in a fall from his kicking horse near the Continental Divide in Alberta. Kicking Horse Pass later became the route of the Canadian Pacific Railway through the Rockies.

13 John N. Lake named Saskatoon after the Cree word for "early berries." According to Lake, "On the first Sunday in August [1882], I was lying in my tent about 3 p.m. when a young man came in with a handful of bright red berries and gave them to me. After eating some, I asked where they were found. He said, 'Along the river bank.' I asked if people had a name for them. He said they were saskatoon berries. I at once exclaimed 'You have found the name of the town.' The

name was formally accepted by the directors that winter and entered in the minutes." Saskatoon berries still grow in the area.

14 Prince Albert, Saskatchewan, is named after Queen Victoria's husband.

15 Prince Edward Island is named after the son of King George III—Queen Victoria's father, Edward, Duke of Kent.

16 Charlottetown, Prince Edward Island, listed as Charlotte Town on the Holland Survey map of 1765, was named for Queen Charlotte (1744–1818), as were the Queen Charlotte Islands.

17 The province of Alberta is named after Queen Victoria's daughter Princess Louise Caroline Alberta, Queen Victoria's fourth daughter and the namesake of Lake Louise. Princess Louise and her husband, Governor General Lord Lorne, travelled across Canada to the Rockies on an 1881 goodwill tour. When Alberta and Saskatchewan joined Confederation in 1905, the people of Alberta selected that name in her honour. Today, there are two bronze statues inside the rotunda of Alberta's Legislature, one of Princess Louise, and one of Blackfoot Chief Crowfoot.

18 Regina, Saskatchewan, and Victoria, British Columbia, are both named after Queen Victoria. The name Regina, Latin for "queen," was assigned to the then town on August 23, 1882, by Governor General Lord Lorne (1845–1914), in honour of his wife's mother, Queen Victoria. Regina was originally called Pile O'Bones, after one of the first cash crops on the Prairies—buffalo bones. First known as Fort Victoria, the capital of British Columbia commemorates Queen Victoria (1819–1901). The name was chosen by the Council of the Northern Department (Hudson's Bay Company) at Fort Garry, June 10, 1843.

19 Victoriaville, Quebec, is famous for its hockey sticks.

20 The name "Ontario" comes from the Iroquois word for "laughing water," or "sparkling water"—a good description of the lake from the north shore.

21 Toronto was originally called York, a name given to it by Governor John Graves Simcoe, who moved the 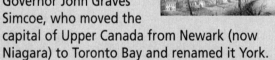 capital of Upper Canada from Newark (now Niagara) to Toronto Bay and renamed it York. In 1834 the city was incorporated as Toronto.

22 The name of the lake, river and capital city of Manitoba comes from the Cree *winnipi* meaning "dirty water" or "murky water." Lake Winnipeg was designated as Sea Lake by David Thompson in 1816.

23 Yellowknife was founded after the discovery of gold in 1934, but its name is derived from the Athapaskan band of Chipewyans, who possessed tools made from yellow copper. Capital of the Northwest Territories, Yellowknife was incorporated as a city January 1, 1970.

24 The capital of Yukon since 1953, Whitehorse was named after the nearby Whitehorse Rapids, which resemble the mane of a white horse.

25 In 1669, La Salle travelled west under the mistaken belief he could cross the continent and find a shorter route to China. His failed exploits led to the derisive labelling of his land as "Lachine." Another version has Jacques Cartier naming the nearby rapids Lachine, after the Iroquois told him of a large body of water to the west, which he interpreted as being the Pacific Ocean.

26 Sydney, Nova Scotia, on Cape Breton Island was named after Thomas Townshend, first Viscount Sydney and British Home Secretary. Sydney, Australia, was also named after Townshend.

27 The Saint John River was given that name by the du Gua-Champlain expedition after its date of discovery, the feast of St. John the Baptist, June 24, 1604. Pierre du Gua, Sieur de Monts, was Samuel de Champlain's patron and a holder of a trade monopoly in New France. He first visited the St. Lawrence as early as 1603 and explored parts of the east coast with Champlain. The Maliseet First Nations originally called the river Wolastoq— "the good river."

28 Brandon, Manitoba, takes its name from the Hudson's Bay Company trading post,

Brandon House, originally built at the junction of the Souris and Assiniboine rivers in 1793.

29 The name "Moose Jaw" appears in the journals of Palliser (1857) and Settee (1861). Settee, an ordained First Nations clergyman, called the place "Moose Jaw Bone," possibly after the shape of the bend in the nearby creek.

30 North Battleford, Saskatchewan, is the name of the town across the river from Battleford. When the town was named, the residents of North Battleford preferred Riverview for a name, and the residents of Battleford protested, fearing the adoption of "their" name for the new town site would draw trade away. They were right, and today's Battleford is almost a museum town, with all the business around the train station across the river.

31 Calgary is a Gaelic word meaning "clear running water." In 1876, Lieutenant-Colonel James Macleod of the North West Mounted Police named the site of his proposed Bow River police post Calgary, the name of the ancestral estate of his cousins, the MacKenzies, on the Isle of Mull, Scotland. Apparently an Inspector Brisebois wanted to name the place after himself but Macleod prevailed.

1 The endangered species the whooping crane breeds in the world's largest national park on the Alberta–Northwest Territories border. What is the name of this park?

2 The longest covered bridge in the world, northwest of Fredericton, New Brunswick, is over what body of water?

3 What is the name of the peninsula on which St. John's, Newfoundland, is located?

4 Windsor, Ontario, and Detroit, Michigan, are connected by the Ambassador Bridge. What two cities are connected by the Rainbow Bridge?

5 In which city can you find a street called Ragged Ass Road?
A. Vancouver
B. Whitehorse
C. Winnipeg
D. Yellowknife

6 Name the province where drivers are not allowed to make a right-hand turn at a red light.

7 "Land of Living Skies" is the slogan on licence plates from which province or territory?
A. Yukon
B. Manitoba
C. Saskatchewan
D. Alberta

8 Which is bigger, Nunavut or Quebec?

9 What small area of West Coast forest has become a battleground between loggers and conservationists?

10 What is Canada's largest ecosystem?
A. Barren land
B. Boreal forest
C. Grassland
D. Tundra

11 Which is the only rat species native to Canada?
A. Brown rat
B. Norway rat
C. Etruscan black rat
D. Bushy-tailed woodrat

12 Where is the longest continuous bridge over sea in the world?

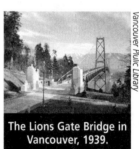

The Lions Gate Bridge in Vancouver, 1939.

Vancouver Plulic Library

13 What rock formation is called the "Sleeping Giant" and where is it found?

14 Ontario is almost twice the size of what European country?

15 What province passed a law in 1908 banning the use of cars in the province?

16 The Trans-Canada Highway is the longest national highway in the world. A 7,821-kilometre (4,860 mi.) road from St. John's, Newfoundland, to Victoria, British Columbia, it was begun on April 25, 1950. On September 3, 1962, Prime Minister Diefenbaker opened the longest paved road in the world in a ceremony at Rogers Pass, Glacier National Park, even though the Ontario section, from Fort Frances east to Atikokan, was not opened until June 28, 1965. Going west, the Trans-Canada Highway divides into the Superior Route and the Northern Route in what city?

17 Give or take 500 kilometres, how long is the drive between Halifax and Vancouver?

18 What's the longest designated street in the world?

19 What do the names Crowsnest, Kicking Horse and Yellowhead have in common?

20 In 1942, over 1,500 miles of road was built between Dawson Creek, British Columbia, and Fairbanks, Alaska, in nine months to create the Alaska Highway. Why was it built?

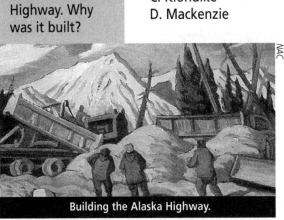

Building the Alaska Highway.

21 Where is the Cabot Trail?

22 Most of Canada's early roads followed Indian trails. By 1734 New France had built a stage coach road, La Route du Roy, along the north shore of the St. Lawrence. It took until 1840 for that road to reach Toronto and the 60-kilometre trip took 36 hours, with 24 changes of horses. Where was the first recorded road in Canada?

23 Name North America's only public highway above the Arctic Circle.
A. Alaska
B. Dempster
C. Klondike
D. Mackenzie

North America's only Arctic highway.

Tourism Yukon

24 What province passed a law in 1919 making car drivers switch from driving on the left-hand side of the road to the right?

25 The Yellowhead Highway is Canada's second longest highway, linking Winnipeg to Prince Rupert through the Yellowhead Pass. Where does the Yellowhead Highway meet the Trans-Canada Highway?

26 What is the name of Canada's first national park, founded in November, 1885?

27 Why, in 1922, did France set aside 250 acres of land within its boundaries as a permanent gift to Canada?

28 Each spring, thousands of bird watchers visit this tiny national park on a V-shaped point of land extending into Lake Erie that is a magnet for birds migrating across the lake.

29 What spectacular landforms in Newfoundland's Gros Morne National Park are usually associated with Norway?

30 The Bruce Trail runs along the Niagara Escarpment from the falls to the Bruce Peninsula. Who is the Bruce Trail named after?

31 What town is the birthplace of Norman Bethune?

32 What is Joe Clark's home town in Alberta?

33 Which Canadian city is situated at the highest altitude?

34 The world's first workable electric streetcar system was powered by hydroelectricity from Niagara Falls and invented by Toronto's John Joseph Wright, whose demonstration amazed the crowds at the 1883 Canadian Industrial Exhibition in Toronto. Until Wright's invention, streetcars were not practical, because rain and snow often short-circuited the electric rails buried in the ground. His solution was to use overhead wires with an electric pole connected to the moving car below. What is the only city in Canada that still uses electric street-cars?

35 What Canadian facility was formerly located in Lahr, West Germany?

36 This Nova Scotia city is named after a city in Scotland.

37 This former royal governor of New France is known as the founder of Kingston, Ontario.

38 The Confederation Bridge linking Prince Edward Island with New Brunswick is Canada's longest bridge. Where is Canada's second longest bridge?

39 What do the Quebec and Honeymoon bridges have in common?

40 Name the prairie city sometimes referred to as the City of Bridges.

41 The longest bridge of this type in Canada is found in Souris, Manitoba.

42 Does Canada have any desert regions?

43 Canada's second largest island is Victoria Island at 217,291 square kilometres. What is Canada's largest island?

44 The Arctic Circle runs through which body of water?
A. Baker Lake
B. Great Slave Lake
C. Great Bear Lake
D. Lake Athabasca

45 Where are the Ottawa Islands located?
A. Hudson Bay
B. Gulf of St. Lawrence
C. Lake Superior
D. Beaufort Sea

46 Grouse Mountain is a landmark of what city?
A. Calgary
B. Montreal
C. Thunder Bay
D. Vancouver
E. St. John's

47 Which of these mountain passes was a route to the Klondike Gold Rush?
A. Crowsnest
B. Kicking Horse
C. Rogers
D. White
E. Yellowhead

48 Blackstrap Mountain is the name of the man-made mountain built for the 1971 Winter Games in which province?

49 Mont Tremblant, Saint-Sauveur and Montebello are ski centres in what mountain range?

50 What mountain landform region is found in the Atlantic provinces?

51 What geological formation is joined to the Adirondack Mountains by the Frontenac Axis?

52 Which province or territory has mountains on its official crest?
A. British Columbia
B. Alberta
C. Yukon

53 In which British Columbia park is Whistler Mountain located?

54 Where can you find the largest glacier in the southern Rocky Mountains, visited by thousands every year?

55 Which Canadian flag and coat of arms feature a husky dog?
A. The Yukon
B. Saskatchewan
C. The Northwest Territories

56 What is so odd about Point Roberts in the state of Washington, just south of the 49th parallel?

57 Along which lake is the "Golden Horseshoe" found?

58 Despite a ruling by the Judicial Committee of the Privy Council in 1927, these two provinces continue to dispute their border.

60 In 1872, what company was awarded the contract to build the transcontinental railroad?

61 The Canadian Pacific Railway runs through which two Rocky Mountain passes?

62 Where did Donald Alexander Smith (Lord Strathcona) drive in the last spike of the CPR to complete Canada's first transcontinental railway?

63 In which province can you find Canada's longest railroad tunnel?

64 What was the nickname of the train that ran from Port-aux-Basques to St. John's during the years 1898–1969?

65 The TIBS, or Train Information Braking System, came into use in 1990. It monitors the engine and the whole length of the train, sending data to trackside monitors and centralized dispatch areas. What did the TIBS put out of commission?

66 What is the name of the train that travels from Cochrane to Moosonee?

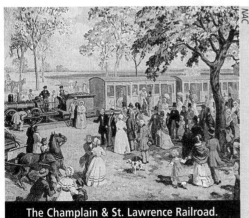

The Champlain & St. Lawrence Railroad.

59 On July 21, 1836, at La Prairie, Quebec, Governor Archibald Acheson, Lord Gosford (1776–1849) rode on the first train of the Champlain & St. Lawrence Railroad. Along with 300 other guests, Lord Gosford was pulled over wooden rails by the first locomotive to run in Canada, the Dorchester. The 23-kilometre line running from La Prairie opposite Montreal to St-Jean-sur-le-Richelieu was Canada's first public railway. It became part of the Montreal and Champlain Railroad in 1857 and was leased to the Grand Trunk in 1864. It is now owned by what modern railway?

121

1 Wood Buffalo National Park, set up in 1922 in Alberta and the Northwest Territories to protect a small remaining herd of wood buffalo, a subspecies of the plains bison, covers 44,807 square kilometres and is Canada's and the world's largest national park.

2 The longest covered bridge in the world is 390.8 metres (1,282 ft.) in length spanning the Saint John River, northwest of Fredericton at Hartland, New Brunswick. It was built between 1897 and 1899.

3 St. John's, Newfoundland, is located on the Avalon Peninsula.

4 The Rainbow Bridge connects Niagara Falls, Ontario, with Niagara Falls, New York.

5 Ragged Ass Road is the name of a road in Yellowknife, Northwest Territories.

6 Drivers are not allowed to make a right-hand turn at a red light in Quebec. In the past few years, motorists in the Outaouais region opposite Ottawa have been allowed to turn on a red light.

7 "Land of Living Skies" is the slogan on Saskatchewan licence plates.

8 The territory of Nunavut, at 1,994,000 square kilometres, is larger than Quebec, Canada's largest province at 1,540,680 square kilometres.

9 Clayoquot Sound, on Vancouver Island, is the largest area of lowland coastal temperate rainforest left in the world and the site of intense disputes between loggers and conservationists.

10 Boreal forest covers 35 per cent of the total area of Canada, making it our country's largest ecosystem.

11 The bushy-tailed woodrat is the only rat native to Canada; all the others are immigrants from Europe.

12 The 12.9-kilometre-long Confederation Bridge, which links Prince Edward Island to New Brunswick, is the longest bridge over sea in the world and has 310 street lights, 17 cameras and 7,500 drainage ports.

13 This island rock formation, which resembles a huge sleeping giant, can be seen from the harbour of Thunder Bay, Ontario.

14 Ontario is almost twice the size of France and three times that of Germany. Ontario could easily fit four United Kingdoms inside its borders.

15 The Prince Edward Island Legislature passed a law in 1908 that forbade anyone from bringing a car into the province.

16 The Trans-Canada Highway divides into the Superior Route and the Northern Route at North Bay, Ontario.

17 The drive from Halifax to Vancouver is about 6,050 kilometres.

18 Before the Trans-Canada Highway was built, the world's longest street used to be Yonge Street, a 1,900.5-kilometre road running north and west from Toronto to Rainy River at the Ontario-Minnesota border. It's still called Yonge Street in the towns it passes through up to Bradford, Ontario, but after Bradford it is called Highway 11. The first 55-kilometre segment of the street was a portage road for the North West Company and was finished in 1796.

19 They are all names of both a Canadian highway and a railway pass through the Canadian Rockies.

20 The Alaska Highway was built in 1942 to move supplies by road into Alaska during World War II. It ends at Fairbanks, Alaska, but most of it runs through Canada. Canada did not take over the Canadian section of the Alaska Highway until 1946.

21 The Cabot Trail is a 296-kilometre highway in Cape Breton, Nova Scotia, noted for its rugged mountain and coastal scenery.

22 The first recorded road in Canada was in Nova Scotia—a bumpy 16-kilometre log-surfaced road built by Champlain in 1606 between Port Royal and Digby.

23 The Dempster Highway runs north from Dawson to Inuvik and is North America's only public highway above the Arctic Circle.

24 In 1919 British Columbia drivers switched to driving on the right-hand side of the road.

25 The Yellowhead Highway meets the Trans-Canada Highway at Portage la Prairie, Manitoba, just west of Winnipeg.

26 Banff National Park in Alberta is Canada's first national park, founded in November 1885. The hot springs that led to its founding were discovered on the mountain near Banff in 1883.

27 The 250-acre site of the Canadian Memorial at Vimy Ridge in France was given to Canada in gratitude for the victory achieved by Canadian troops and the Canadian lives sacrificed in the capture of Vimy Ridge in April 1917 during World War I.

28 Point Pelee National Park on Lake Erie, in southern Ontario, is visited each spring by thousands of bird watchers during the annual bird migration. Pelée, in French, means "bald" or "denuded," a description given to the point by French explorers in the early 1700s.

29 Gros Morne National Park features spectacular fjords.

30 The Bruce Trail and Bruce Peninsula are named after James Bruce, eighth Earl of Elgin. As governor-general of British North America (1847–54), Elgin brought democratically responsible government to Canada. He was later appointed viceroy of India in 1862, and died there a year later.

31 Gravenhurst, Ontario, is the birthplace of Norman Bethune. Parks Canada now operates his boyhood home as a museum.

32 High River is Joe Clark's home town.

33 Rossland, British Columbia, nestled in the crater of an ancient volcano at an elevation of 1,023 metres above sea level, is Canada's highest city.

34 Toronto is the only city in Canada still operating electric streetcars.

35 A Canadian Armed Forces Base was formerly located in Lahr, Germany.

36 New Glasgow, Nova Scotia, is named after a Scottish city.

37 Count Frontenac is the founder of Kingston, Ontario.

38 The Pierre Laporte Bridge (670 metres long) connects Quebec City to the south shore of the St. Lawrence River and is Canada's second-lowest after the Confederation Bridge.

39 Both the Quebec and Honeymoon bridges collapsed: the Quebec Bridge in 1907, Niagara Falls' Honeymoon Bridge in 1938.

40 Saskatoon is sometimes called the City of Bridges.

41 The longest footbridge in Canada is in Souris, Manitoba.

42 Canada is home to one of the largest desert areas in the world—the tundras of the Northwest Territories and Nunavik contain large areas that receive less than 250 millimetres of annual precipitation.

43 Baffin Island is Canada's largest island. At 507,451 square kilometres it is the fourth largest island in the world.

44 The Arctic Circle runs through Great Bear Lake.

45 The Ottawa Islands are in Hudson Bay.

46 Grouse Mountain looms above North Vancouver, just 15 minutes from downtown via The Skyride, North America's largest aerial tramway.

47 Prospectors travelled to Skagway, Alaska, by boat and then climbed over the White Pass to the Yukon gold fields.

48 Blackstrap Mountain is in Saskatchewan.

49 Mont Tremblant, Saint-Sauveur and Montebello are all in the Laurentians.

50 The Appalachian mountains are in New Brunswick.

51 The Canadian Shield, Canada's largest geological formation, is joined to the Adirondack Mountains by the Frontenac Axis.

52 The province of Alberta has mountains on its official crest.

53 Whistler Mountain is in Garibaldi Provincial Park.

54 The Columbia Icefield contains the largest glacier in the southern Rocky Mountains.

55 A husky dog is featured on the flag and coat of arms of the Yukon.

56 Americans travelling by car to Point Roberts can only visit this part of Washington State by first crossing the border into Canada. Although located at the end of a peninsula which is Canadian, Point Roberts, at the southern tip, is south of the 49th parallel and is, therefore, part of Washington State.

57 Lake Ontario. It's the horseshoe-shaped area from Niagara to Oshawa.

58 Newfoundland and Quebec still dispute their border. Newfoundland offered to sell the territory of Labrador to Quebec during the Depression, but the price was thought too high.

59  Canada's first public railway is now part of the rail system owned by CN (Canadian National).

60 The Canadian Pacific Railway Company was awarded the contract to build the transcontinental railroad in 1872. The engineer responsible was an Illinois Central railway builder named William Cornelius Van Horne who renounced his American citizenship and became a Canadian citizen after its completion.

61 The Canadian Pacific Railway runs through Kicking Horse Pass and Rogers Pass.

62 The famous last spike was driven in at Craigellachie, BC. The place was named after the war cry of Smith's family, the clan Grant—"Stand fast, Craigellachie."

63 The Rogers Pass tunnel in British Columbia, Canada's longest, is approximately eight kilometres long.

64 The slow train that once ran across the province was affectionately known as the Newfie Bullet.

65 Before the TIBS, every freight train in Canada used to pull a caboose at its end. The caboose contained a kitchen and bunks for the train crew and a viewing window on top for watching for sparks or other mechanical problems along the length of the train.

66 The train from Cochrane to Moosonee is called the Polar Bear Express.

CANADA BY AIR AND SEA

1 Which flying creature performs one of the world's great annual migrations from Canada to Mexico?

2 Which Canadian bird makes the longest migration?
A. Canada goose
B. Whooping crane
C. Arctic tern

A DeHavilland 9A (G-CYBF) on the first cross-Canada flight.

3 Which bird is the largest owl in Canada and North America?
A. Snowy owl
B. Great horned owl
C. Northern hawk owl
D. Great grey owl

4 What is the name of the dry, warm wind that blows down the eastern slopes of the Rocky Mountains in Alberta?

5 Air Force captain Brian A. Peck made the first official airmail flight in Canada on June 24, 1918, taking the mail from Montreal to Toronto. What Toronto-built plane carried the world's first airmail by jet on April 18, 1950?

6 Who was the first Canadian to fly across the Rockies?

National Aviation Museum

7 The first cross-Canada airplane flights were relays made by the Canadian Air Force in October 1920. Crews left Halifax, Nova Scotia, on October 7 flying the Fairey seaplane. At Winnipeg, Manitoba, the seaplanes and flying boats used throughout the eastern leg of the journey were replaced by three DeHavilland 9As of which only one (G-CYBF) finally made it to Vancouver, British Columbia. The total flying time was 49 hours, 7 minutes. How many days did the trip take?

8 Pilots Billy Wells and Maurice McGregor were at the controls when a Lockheed 10A Electra aircraft lifted off the runway in Vancouver on its way to Seattle. This was Air Canada's first flight; when did it happen?

9 What 1922 invention by Wallace Turnbull (1870–1954) of Rothesay, New Brunswick, helped revolutionize the aircraft industry?

10 This airline was formed in 1942 by amalgamating 10 smaller airlines operating in the west and north.

11 An Air Canada DC-8 crashed in Toronto on its landing approach, on July 5, 1970, resulting in 109 deaths. This same type of plane was involved in the worst air crash on Canadian soil. When and where did it occur?

12 In 1919, Frank Ellis became the first Canadian to use this method of debarking a plane.

13 What Canadian airport has the largest landing surface in the world?

14 On June 14, 1919, British Army captain John Alcock and Lieutenant Arthur Brown took off from Lester's Field at St. John's, Newfoundland, in their Vickers Vimy bomber, a two-motor biplane. Where did they land?

15 What caused the September 2, 1998, crash of a Swissair flight from New York to Geneva, and where did it go down?

16 What monster, a distant and not so famous relation of the Loch Ness Monster, is said to live in Okanagan Lake, British Columbia?

17 Where is the oldest working lighthouse in Canada?

18 Into what sea does the Yukon River flow?

21 Name the five types of Pacific salmon caught on Canada's West Coast.

NAC

A British Columbia fishing fleet.

19 What body of water separates Greenland from Canada?

20 Which of the following bodies of water is not linked to Hudson Bay?
A. Bathurst Inlet
B. Chesterfield Inlet
C. Dawson Inlet
D. Rankin Inlet

22 What tiny mollusk was first introduced to Canada in 1988 and has since become a significant pest throughout the waters of the Great Lakes and the St. Lawrence basin?

23 Canada claims sovereignty over its ocean waters up to how many nautical miles offshore?

24 Which of the three following provinces has an ocean shoreline?
A. Saskatchewan
B. Ontario
C. Alberta

25 Hudson Bay is the largest bay in the world. How long is its shoreline?
A. 12,268 kilometres
B. 122,680 kilometres
C. 226,800 kilometres

26 How old are the Greenland icebergs, and how many get to the Grand Banks off Newfoundland every year?

27 In what year did the St. Lawrence Seaway open?

28 Name the Canadian who invented the screw propeller for ships.

29 Which province has the most salt water coastline, British Columbia or Newfoundland?

30 An RCMP ship named the *St. Roch*, captained by Henry Larsen, was first to cross this passage in both directions.

31 What was the name of Canada's last aircraft carrier, sold for scrap in 1972?

32 Canada's first steamboat made its debut in 1809. What was its name?
A. *Accommodation*
B. *Empress of Canada*
C. *Royal William*

RCMP officer Henry Larsen on the *St. Roch* in 1944.

NAC

A steamboat on the Saskatchewan River near Medicine Hat.

NAC

33 The first ship to cross the Atlantic under steam power was the *Royal William*. Built at Cape Blanc, Quebec, by George Black and John Saxton Campbell for a Quebec company, the 830-ton ship was launched on Friday, April 29, 1831, in the presence of Governor Lord Aylmer and christened by Lady Aylmer after the reigning king. Under the command of Captain McDougall, she left Quebec August 4, 1833, and arrived at Gravesend, September 11. After her trip she was sold in London to the Spanish government as a warship or transport. What route was the *Royal William* originally intended to serve?

34 In 1946, an editorial in the *Globe and Mail* read, "The lithe, graceful Queen of the Grand Banks who once danced the waves on slippered feet, died plodding a weary path. ... That she fell from glory to the ignoble job of her last three years was no credit to Canada." What was the *Globe* referring to?

35 In early nineteenth-century Quebec, a 3,700-ton wooden vessel was made of squared timbers held together by removable pegs. On its maiden voyage, a mid-Atlantic storm popped out the pegs, and all hands were lost. Why was such a boat built?

36 Niagara Falls is on the Niagara River, which flows between Lake Erie and Lake Ontario. What canal allows ships to bypass the falls?

37 What is the name of the boat that tours below the Niagara Falls?

38 Name the two islands in the Gulf of St. Lawrence that represent France's last colonial holdings in North America.

39 What is Île St-Jean's modern name?

40 Which is larger—Vancouver Island or Prince Edward Island?

41 What is the name of the body of water that separates Cape Breton Island from Nova Scotia?
A. Northumberland Strait
B. Strait of Belle Isle
C. Strait of Canso
D. Georgia Strait

42 This island is the home of Pacific Rim National Park.

43 This Lake Huron island is the largest fresh water island in the world.

44 Alert is Canada's most northern settlement. On what island is it located?

45 Graham and Moresby are the names of the two major islands in what Pacific chain?

46 What natural event shut down Niagara Falls on March 29, 1848?

47 The largest areas of Canada are drained by rivers flowing into which ocean?
A. The Arctic
B. The Pacific
C. The Atlantic and Hudson Bay

48 What large river has its source in the United States yet most of its flow in Canada?

49 In what city are the Reversing Falls Rapids?

50 Which ocean receives the most water by volume from Canadian rivers?
A. The Arctic
B. The Pacific
C. The Atlantic and Hudson Bay

51 In 1960, the SS *Keno* made the last sternwheeler trip down this river in Canada's North.

52 Approximately how much of the world's fresh water is in Canada?
A. 7 per cent
B. 15 per cent
C. 22 per cent
D. 30 per cent

129

1 The Monarch butterfly travels from Canada to northern Mexico every year.

2 The Arctic tern (*Sterna paradisaea*) is a small bird that makes the longest migration of any bird in Canada. It breeds in the Arctic tundra (within the Arctic Circle), but flies to the edge of the Antarctic ice pack during the winter—a round trip of 35,000 kilometres each year—roughly the circumference of the Earth.

3 The great grey owl (*Strix nebulosa*) is the largest owl in Canada. Also called the great grey ghost, spruce owl, bearded owl and sooty owl, it is the provincial bird of Manitoba and can reach a wingspan of 140 centimetres.

4 The chinook is the warm wind that blows down from the Rocky Mountains.

5 The Avro jetliner, designed in Canada by engineer James Floyd, made the world's first airmail delivery by jet. In a 75-minute flight in April 1950, the Avro Jetliner completed the first international jet transport flight in North America, carrying mail from Toronto to New York. When the plane first flew on August 10, 1949, over Downsview airport in Toronto, it was the first flight of a jet transport in North America, and the second in the world, only two weeks after the British Comet. James Floyd later won the Wright Medal for aviation innovation, the first non-American to win the award.

6 Captain Ernest C. Hoy became the first to fly across the Canadian Rockies in August 1919 when, after zigzagging through mountain passes, barely scraping the treetops and being buffeted by strong winds, he landed in Calgary 16 hours and 42 minutes after taking off from Vancouver.

7 The first cross-Canada airplane trip finished in Vancouver on October 17, 1920, after 11 days, having covered 3,265 miles.

8 On September 1, 1937, Trans-Canada Airlines' first-ever commercial flight took place departing Vancouver for Seattle. Flights across Canada started in April 1939 when regular Trans-Canada Airline (TCA) passenger service in Lockheed Electras began from Vancouver to Montreal and points in between. The flight took more than a day and passengers had to wear oxygen masks part of the time. All the flight attendants had to be professional nurses, unmarried, and under 5'5".

9 The variable-pitch or controlled-pitch propeller was invented by Wallace Turnbull. This invention alone created the air transportation industry, since it made it possible for aircraft to get off the ground carrying larger payloads and to get them economically to distant destinations. The Turnbull propeller was first flight-tested by the Canadian Air Force in 1927 on an Avro biplane. Turnbull also invented the world's first wind tunnel.

10 Canadian Pacific Airlines was formed in 1942 from 10 smaller airlines.

11 On November 29, 1963, Trans-Canada Airlines DC-8F crashed near Ste-Thérèse, Quebec, after taking off from Dorval. All 118 aboard died in the worst air crash on Canadian soil.

12 Frank Ellis was the first Canadian to jump from a plane wearing a parachute in 1919.

13 Mirabel, northwest of Montreal, has the largest landing surface of any airport in the world.

14 John Alcock and Arthur Brown were the first to make a nonstop transatlantic flight. Their 3,100-kilometre flight ended 16 hours later with a nose-down landing in Clifden, County Galway, Ireland, in a peat bog. They won the £10,000 prize offered by the *London Daily Mail*, and were both awarded knighthoods.

15 Swissair Flight 111 crashed off Peggy's Cove, Nova Scotia, killing all 229 aboard the McDonnell Douglas MD-11 on September 2, 1998. Faulty wiring was blamed.

16 The monster of Lake Okanagan goes by the name Ogopogo.

17 Canada's oldest working lighthouse is Fisgard Lighthouse, built in 1873 and located a few kilometres from Victoria, British Columbia.

18 The Yukon River flows into the Bering Sea.

19 Davis Strait separates Greenland from Canada.

20 Bathurst Inlet connects to the Arctic Ocean, but not to Hudson Bay.

21 Chinook, chum, coho, pink and sockeye are the five types of Pacific salmon.

22 The zebra mussel was introduced into Lake Erie by a European freighter in 1988. It has now settled comfortably into much of the St. Lawrence drainage basin, where it munches plankton, clogs drainage pipes and slashes the toes of unwary swimmers with its sharp edges.

23 Canada's offshore limit is 200 nautical miles. Through a claim to a commission of the United Nations, Canada is seeking to have its current 200 nautical mile offshore limit expanded by over 150 miles in some areas of Atlantic Canada in order to manage fish stocks and offshore oil drilling. The claim under international law is asking that Canada be given new jurisdiction over an area of ocean floor roughly equivalent to the three Prairie provinces.

24 Ontario has an ocean shoreline on James and Hudson bays.

25 Hudson Bay has a shoreline 12,268 kilometres long (7,623 mi.) and an area of 1,233,000 square kilometres or 476,000 square miles.

26 Most Greenland icebergs are about 3,000 years old, and each spring about 30,000 of them break away from the ice fields along the west coast of Greenland and start drifting south, taking about three months to reach Newfoundland. In an average summer, about 500 reach the Grand Banks. Heavy iceberg years actually diminish the warmth of the Gulf Stream and cause colder summers in Europe.

27 The St. Lawrence Seaway opened in 1959.

28 In 1833, Nova Scotian John Patch (1789–1861) began testing his new marine propeller, which literally left other propellers in its wake. He wanted to register a patent in the United States for his screw propeller, but was talked out of it, only to learn several years later that his idea had been put into practice in England.

29 British Columbia has the longest salt water coastline, 26,000 kilometres in total distance.

30 Between 1940 and 1942, RCMP officer Henry Larsen sailed the Royal Canadian Mounted Police patrol schooner, the *St. Roch*, built in North Vancouver, through the Northwest Passage from west to east, repeating the 1903–06 feat of Norwegian Roald Amundsen. In 1944, Larsen sailed the passage again by a more northerly route through the Arctic Archipelago in only 86 days, becoming the first vessel to travel the passage west to east, and in both directions. In 1950 Larsen sailed the same boat through the Panama Canal to Halifax, making her the first vessel to circumnavigate North America. The *St. Roch* was purchased by the City of Vancouver in 1954; the ship is now on permanent display at the Maritime Museum. In 1969, the oil tanker *Manhattan* became the first commercial ship to sail the Northwest Passage.

31 Canada's last aircraft carrier was named the HMCS *Bonaventure*.

32 The *Accommodation* was Canada's first steamboat, built by William Molson for use on the St. Lawrence in 1809. It travelled between Quebec and Montreal.

33 The *Royal William* was built to run between Quebec and Halifax, but her owners chose instead to make the first steam-powered transatlantic passage. Many Americans still claim that the first steamer to cross the Atlantic was the *Savannah*, which in 1819 made the voyage from Georgia to Liverpool in 25 days. The *Savannah*, however, was not a steamship, and was under sail more than two-thirds of the way across. She was a full-rigged packet ship, and had on her deck a small steam engine to push her along when the wind failed.

The original Bluenose on a commemorative stamp.

34 The *Globe* editorial of 1946 was referring to the original *Bluenose*, the fishing schooner featured on the Canadian dime. Built for the then unheard of figure of $35,000, and launched in 1921, the Bluenose was designed to race and catch fish. The ship was unbeatable, but her final years weren't happy, and when her captain, Angus Walters, tried to raise money to have her declared a national treasure, there were no takers and he was forced to sell her as a West Indies freighter. The *Bluenose* sank off the coast of Haiti in 1946.

35 In the early 1800s, squared timber fetched a high price in England, so the British taxed it heavily. But there was no tax on wooden ships, so a Quebec City entrepreneur named McPherson decided to sail around the British tax collectors by building a recyclable ship, one that could be dismantled and sold off for its timber. Unfortunately, his scheme proved a disaster.

36 The Welland Canal allows ships to bypass Niagara Falls. First opened in 1829, it has undergone a series of improvements over the years.

37 The *Maid of the Mist* tours below the Niagara Falls.

38 St. Pierre and Miquelon are the last French holdings in North America and are still the territory of France.

39 Nicknamed the Garden of the Gulf, Prince Edward Island was known as Île St-Jean until 1763.

40 Vancouver Island is larger than Prince Edward Island.

41 The Strait of Canso separates Cape Breton Island and Nova Scotia.

42 Pacific Rim National Park is found on Vancouver Island.

43 The largest fresh water island in the world is Manitoulin Island, at 2,766 square kilometres.

44 Alert, Northwest Territories, is on Ellesmere Island.

45 Graham and Moresby islands are both among the Queen Charlotte Islands.

46 The Niagara River stopped flowing over Niagara Falls in March 1848 because ice lodged in the river at the inlet from Lake Erie. The ice dam lasted for two days; then, on the night of March 31, a change in the weather and winds uncorked the ice and a sudden surge of water swept down the riverbed and over the falls.

47 The largest areas of Canada are drained into the Arctic Ocean.

48 The Columbia River rises in the US Rockies, then runs north and turns south through British Columbia and the state of Washington to the Pacific Ocean.

49 The Reversing Falls Rapids are in Saint John, New Brunswick. They stop flowing and start falling upstream when the huge Bay of Fundy tide enters the narrow channel of the Saint John River.

50 The Arctic Ocean receives more water from Canadian rivers than any other ocean, largely from the Mackenzie River.

51 The Yukon River is where the last sternwheeler riverboat sailed in Canada in 1960.

52 Canada has approximately 15 per cent of the world's fresh water.

A glacier in the Rocky Mountains.

1 The greatest snowfall in Canada happens on Mount Fidelity in Glacier National Park, British Columbia, with 1,433 millimetres falling in the average year. On average, what is the snowiest town in Canada?
A. Lakelse Lake, British Columbia
B. Corner Brook, Newfoundland
C. Sept-Îles, Quebec
D. Ottawa, Ontario

2 Where in Canada would you find the world's largest teepee?

3 What is the longest river in Canada?

4 What is the highest mountain in Canada, at almost 6,000 metres?

5 Which of these three Prairie cities is at the highest altitude?
A. Saskatoon, Saskatchewan
B. Edmonton, Alberta
C. Brandon, Manitoba

6 What is the driest city in Canada?
A. Brandon, Manitoba
B. Medicine Hat, Alberta
C. Regina, Saskatchewan

7 What is the highest mountain in Canada outside the Yukon?
A. Mount Robson, British Columbia
B. Mount Columbia, Alberta
C. Fairweather Mountain, British Columbia

8 Who is Mount Logan named after?

9 What is the highest waterfall in Canada?

10 What Canadian location received the most precipitation in a single year?

11 The Nakwakto Rapids at Slingsby Channel in British Columbia are the strongest currents in the world. How fast are they?
A. 25 kilometres per hour
B. 30 kilometres per hour
C. 50 kilometres per hour
D. 55 kilometres per hour

12 Where in Canada can you find the highest tides in the world and the location of the only tidal power plant in the Western hemisphere?

Low tide at the location of the highest tides in the world.

13 Which of these three Canadian lakes is *not* on the list of the world's 10 deepest lakes?
A. Lake Superior
B. Great Bear Lake
C. Lake Huron

The Great Lakes seen from space.

NASA

14 Which of the Great Lakes is the shallowest?

15 What is the deepest lake in Canada?

16 *Castor canadensis* is Canada's largest rodent and was almost extinct in the early twentieth century. What is its common name?

17 What Canadian bird has the longest wingspan?
A. Whooping crane
B. Albatross
C. White pelican

18 Which province is home to the most mammal and bird species in Canada?

19 What Canadian resident is the world's largest carnivorous land mammal? Wapusk National Park was created partly to protect its breeding grounds.

20 The coldest temperature ever recorded in Canada was an estimate because it was colder than the lowest mark on the thermometer. Where was the coldest-ever temperature in Canada recorded?
A. Snag, Yukon
B. Resolute, Northwest Territories
C. Fort Chimo, Quebec
D. Pelly Bay, Northwest Territories

21 The area of the Northwest Territories that includes Ellesmere Island, Axel Heiberg Island and the Boothia Peninsula experiences average January temperatures of −35 °C or lower and is the coldest region in Canada. What is the coldest city in Canada?

22 Where was the coldest-ever wind chill temperature recorded in Canada?
A. Resolute, Northwest Territories
B. Fort Chimo, Quebec
C. Pelly Bay, Northwest Territories

23 What part of Canada receives the most sunshine daily?

24 Among Canada's 75 largest cities, which has the shortest frost-free period?
A. Red Deer, Alberta
B. Sept-Îles, Quebec
C. Prince Rupert, British Columbia
D. Thompson, Manitoba

25 One Canadian province holds three different records concerning weather: Canada's sunniest city or town, the heaviest rainfall in Canada in a one-hour period and Canada's highest recorded temperature. Which province holds these three records?

26 What is the thunderstorm capital of Canada?

135

1 According to Natural Resources Canada, Corner Brook, Newfoundland, is the snowiest city, with an annual average snowfall of 414 centimetres. However, Environment Canada says Sept-Îles, Quebec, is the snowiest city in Canada. It also says, "Charlottetown's 330.6 cm makes it the third snowiest city next to St. John's and Quebec." Which government department is right? Moncton, New Brunswick, also claims the prize. On March 7, 1999, Moncton had a one-day snowdump of 116 centimetres (45.7 in.).

2 The world's largest teepee is in Medicine Hat, Alberta.

3 The Mackenzie River is the longest river in Canada, flowing from Lake Athabasca in Alberta to the Beaufort Sea. It is one of the world's longest at 4,241 kilometres.

4 Mount Logan in southwestern Yukon is Canada's highest peak, at 5,959 metres.

5 Edmonton, at 666.3 metres (2,186 ft.) above sea level, is higher than Saskatoon or Brandon.

6 Medicine Hat, Alberta, is Canada's driest city with, on average, 271 dry days a year.

7 At 4,663 metres, Fairweather Mountain, British Columbia, near the Yukon border is the highest mountain in Canada outside the Yukon.

8 Mount Logan is named after Sir William Edmond Logan, who founded the Geological Survey of Canada in 1842.

9 Della Falls, British Columbia, is the highest waterfall in Canada, with a 440-metre vertical drop.

10 In 1931, Henderson Lake, British Columbia, received 812 centimetres of precipitation, the highest annual rainfall recorded in Canada.

11 The flow of the Nakwakto Rapids at Slingsby Channel in British Columbia can reach a rate of 16 knots or 30 kilometres per hour.

12 The highest tides on Earth are in the Minas Basin at the eastern extremity of the Bay of Fundy where the average change from low tide to high tide is 12 metres and can reach 16 metres when the various factors affecting the tides are in phase. The gravitational pull of the moon and sun raises the tides, but much of the energy comes from the rotational energy of the earth spinning on its axis. Near Annapolis Royal, Nova Scotia, the only tidal power plant in the Western hemisphere generates 20 megawatts at peak, about one per cent of the province's electrical power capacity.

13 Lake Huron is not one of the world's 10 deepest lakes.

14 Lake Erie is the shallowest of the Great Lakes, with a maximum depth of 65 metres and an average depth of less than 20 metres.

15 Great Slave Lake is 615 metres deep, the deepest lake in Canada.

16 The common name for *Castor canadensis* is the beaver.

17 The white pelican has a wingspan of three metres.

18 British Columbia is home to the highest number of mammal and bird species in Canada. One hundred and nineteen of Canada's 209 mammals and 362 of the 462 species of birds resident in Canada are in British Columbia.

19 The adult male polar bear can weigh up to 600 kilograms (1,320 lb.) and have a nose to tail measurement of 2.6 metres (8 ft., 6 in.). It is the world's largest carnivorous animal and its primary prey is the seal, but it also eats fish, seaweed, grass and the occasional caribou.

20 On February 3, 1947, thermometers at the airstrip at Snag, Yukon, registered –64 °C (–83 °F), the lowest temperature recorded in Canada and likely the lowest temperature on record in North America. This record was an estimate, since thermometers in use were only graduated to 80 degrees below zero, and the gauges registered below the lowest mark. According to Environment Canada, Gordon Toole, the weather observer at Snag who checked the thermometer that day, said his breath hissed as he was breathing and formed a vapour trail behind him.

21 Yellowknife is the coldest city in Canada, with a mean annual temperature of –5.4 °C.

22 At Pelly Bay in the Northwest Territories the temperature on January 13, 1975, was –51 °C, but 50-kilometre winds made it feel like –92 °C, Canada's coldest-ever wind-chill temperature.

23 Southern Saskatchewan and southeastern Alberta each receive approximately 2,400 hours of effective sunshine annually, making this region Canada's sunniest. By contrast, Halifax and Vancouver receive only 1,800 hours and Toronto about 2,000 hours of sunshine.

24 Thompson, Manitoba, has the shortest frost-free period in Canada each year.

25 Saskatchewan holds three amazing weather records. Canada's sunniest town is Estevan, Saskatchewan, with 2,537 hours annually. Canada's most intense rainstorm took place at Buffalo Gap, Saskatchewan, on May 30, 1961, when, according to Environment Canada, over 250 millimetres of rain pelted down in less than an hour. The rain was so strong it even stripped the bark from trees. And both Yellowgrass and Midale, Saskatchewan, share the record for Canada's highest temperature of 45 °C (113 °F), set July 5, 1937.

26 It's a toss-up between Windsor, Ontario, and London, Ontario. Both cities average 34 thunderstorm days per year. That's nothing compared to the thunderstorm capital of the world, Kampala, Uganda, which has 242 thunderstorm days per year.

Celebrities?

Canada Writes

Canada Entertains

Canada Paints

Canada Performs

Canada Laughs

1 What is the name of the town where *Anne of Green Gables* is set?

2 What fictional Canadian town did Margaret Laurence make famous in her novels?

3 What film won the 1997 Academy Award for Best Picture and who is the author of the original book?

4 What famous movie starring Kevin Costner is based on W.P. Kinsella's novel *Shoeless Joe*?

5 Which author's books on woodcraft formed the basis of the first official manual of the Boy Scouts of America?

Author, naturalist and co-founder of the Boy Scouts of America.

6 Which of the following was the first novel written in Canada?
A. *The Theatre of Neptune* by Marc Lescarbot
B. *The History of Emily Montague* by Frances Brooke
C. *The Deserted Village* by Oliver Goldsmith

7 American humorist Mark Twain was greatly influenced by Nova Scotia writer Thomas C. Haliburton (1796–1865). What was the name of Haliburton's famous fictional character?
A. Sam Slick
B. Sam McGee
C. Sam Steele

8 Who were les Plouffe, created by novelist Roger Lemelin?

9 Who wrote *As for Me and My House*?

10 What famous Canadian author wrote a book arguing that "survival" is a major theme of Canadian literature and also wrote the children's book *Princess Prunella and the Purple Peanut*?

11 Which of Gabrielle Roy's novels was made into an award-winning film and was originally published in French with the title *Bonheur d'occasion*?

12 Who wrote the poem "The Cremation of Sam McGee"?

13 Who wrote the novel *Who Has Seen the Wind*, which later became a movie starring Gordon Pinsent?

14 John McCrae's poem "In Flanders Fields" was written during which war?
A. Vietnam
B. World War II
C. Korean War
D. World War I

15 Which Canadian writer coined the term "Generation X" in 1991?
A. Robertson Davies
B. Margaret Atwood
C. Douglas Copeland
D. Leonard Cohen

Library of Congress

16 Who has won the Governor General's Award for Literature the most times?
A. Margaret Atwood
B. Michael Ondaatje
C. Hugh MacLennan
D. Robertson Davies

17 Where was Canadian author Michael Ondaatje born?
A. India
B. Sri Lanka
C. Holland
D. England

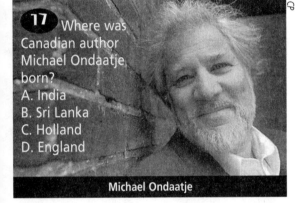
Michael Ondaatje

18 Which author, known for his fiction and commentary, also published the children's book *Jacob Two-Two Meets the Hooded Fang*?

19 What is the name of the fictional Saskatchewan poet immortalized by Paul Hiebert as the Prairie Songstress?

20 Who was Evangeline?

21 Englishman Archibald Belaney moved to Canada in 1905 to live with the Native people and devote his life to nature. He became a well-known author and conservationist under what name?

Archibald Belaney, 1888–1938 *(NAC)*

22 In 1914, army veterinarian Harry Colebourn bought a bear cub at White River, Ontario, and named her after a Canadian city. This bear later gave its name to a character in a famous series of children's books. What is the name of the city and the bear's fictional namesake?

23 Name the author who was barred from entering the United States in 1985 because his name was listed in a US "Lookout book" as an "undesirable"?
A. Mordecai Richler
B. Pierre Elliot Trudeau
C. Farley Mowat
D. Pierre Vallieres

24 Name the Nobel Prize–winning author who worked for the *Toronto Star* in the 1920s and was beaten in a boxing match in Paris by Canadian author Morley Callaghan.

25 *Maria Chapdelaine* is a famous Canadian novel by Louis Hémon about the difficulties of nineteenth-century pioneer life. Where was he born?

26 What is Anne of Green Gables' last name?

27 In what province did Lucy Maud Montgomery write the majority of her "Anne" novels?

28 Name the author of *Roughing It in the Bush* and *Life in the Clearings*, two books published in the 1850s that documented the struggles of pioneer women.

29 Named after the last of Canada's official executioners, what is the Arthur Ellis Award?

Stephen Leacock, 1869–1944

30 What is the model for the town of Mariposa in Stephen Leacock's 1912 *Sunshine Sketches of a Little Town*?

Leacock Residence, Old Brewery Bay

31 What Canadian won Britain's richest literary prize, the Orange Prize for fiction, in 1997?
A. Carol Shields
B. Anne Michaels
C. Jane Urquhart
D. Margaret Atwood

32 Which British poet referred to Canada as "Our Lady of the Snows"?
A. Robert Browning
B. Rudyard Kipling
C. Robert Louis Stevenson
D. Alfred, Lord Tennyson

33 Under the pseudonym Franklin W. Dixon, Leslie McFarlane, born in Whitby, Ontario, started what famous series of mystery books for young boys?

34 What Canadian publisher is the largest paperback publisher in the world?

35 Who is the writer of the Benny Cooperman mystery series set in Ontario?
A. Alison Gordon
B. Howard Engel
C. Ellen Godfrey
D. Peter Robinson

36 What is Canada's richest literary award?
A. Booker Prize
B. Governor General's Award
C. Giller Prize
D. National Book Award

37 What Newfoundland poet wrote the epic poems "The Cachalot" (1926), "The Titanic" (1935) and "Towards the Last Spike" (1952)?

38 Richard Dreyfuss starred in the movie version of this Mordecai Richler book.

39 Earle Birney, Al Purdy and Alden Nowlan are all known for what type of writing?

40 Who wrote *Malice in Blunderland*?

41 Under what pseudonym did Don Harron write *Jogfree of Canada*?

42 Who is the author of the trilogy that comprises *Fifth Business*, *The Manticore* and *World of Wonders*?

43 Writer of poetry, novels, short stories, and television scripts, his play *The Ecstasy of Rita Joe* highlighted the plight of Canadian Native people. Who is he?

44 A memorial medal, named after this author, is given annually for the best Canadian book of humour.

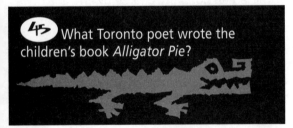

45 What Toronto poet wrote the children's book *Alligator Pie*?

46 Her two-volume autobiography is entitled *Beyond Reason* and *Consequences*.

47 She is the author of the novel *La Belle Bete*, published in English as *Mad Shadows*.

48 This journalist and member of the Order of Canada wrote *You Can't Print That*. He also conducted the Coolbrook Symphony on the opening night of the National Arts Centre. What is his name?

49 Robin Philips directed the screen version of which Governor General Award–winning novel by Timothy Findley?

50 Name the Montreal publisher who printed the first halftone engravings in his newspaper.

The Eye Opener.

The inaugural issue of *The Eye Opener.*

51 What Canadian nature magazine is named for the two times of year when the sun crosses the equator and day and night are of equal length?

52 What popular back-to-the-land magazine is named after the Ontario town where it originates?

53 In 1969, Robert Fulford became the editor of what long-time cultural and literary magazine?

54 What is Canada's largest newspaper by circulation?
A. *The Globe and Mail*
B. *The Toronto Star*
C. *La Presse*
D. *The National Post*

55 In 1902, who founded and ran the legendary Alberta newspaper known as *The Eye Opener*?

56 Lord Beaverbrook, Lord Thomson of Fleet and Lord Black of Crossharbour are British titles given to three Canadian-born newspaper barons. What are their names?

57 This cooperative news service, supplying most of Canada's newspapers, started operations in 1917.

58 What is the name of Montreal's daily English newspaper?

59 Claude Ryan was once the editor of this newspaper.

1 *Anne of Green Gables* is set in Cavendish, Prince Edward Island.

2 Manawaka, a fictional town based on Neepawa, Manitoba, is the setting for several of the novels of Margaret Laurence.

3 *The English Patient* by Michael Ondaatje won Canada's Governor General's Award for fiction and the Booker Award (shared) in Britain 1992. In 1997, the movie *The English Patient* won the Academy Award for Best Picture.

4 *Field of Dreams* is based on the novel *Shoeless* Joe by W.P. Kinsella.

5 In 1910, naturalist Ernest Thompson Seton (1860–1946) helped Daniel Bears and Lord Baden-Powell in the founding of the Boy Scouts of America. Seton was born in South Shields, England, and settled with his parents at Lindsay, Ontario. A graduate of the Ontario College of Art in 1879, he homesteaded in Manitoba, then moved to the USA in 1896. Two years later, Seton published his first book of illustrated animal stories, *Wild Animals I Have Known*, which was an instant success. In 1915 he was expelled from the Boy Scouts organization, after quarrelling with Baden-Powell about what he considered to be its militaristic stance. He spent the remainder of his life studying nature, writing extensively on Manitoba and subarctic wildlife, and set up the Seton Village for children's nature study in Santa Fe, New Mexico.

6 Frances Brooke's *The History of Emily Montague*, published in 1769, was the first novel written in Canada by either a man or a women. An essayist, novelist and playwright, Brooke spent most of her life in London, but lived in Quebec for five years with her army chaplain husband.

7 Yankee peddler Sam Slick is the fictional character made famous by Thomas C. Haliburton.

8 Roger Lemelin's les Plouffe, from the novel of the same name, were a fictional French Canadian family in Quebec City. The novel was turned into a long-running television series in Quebec, as well as a film.

9 *As for Me and My House* is by Sinclair Ross.

10 Margaret Atwood's *Survival: A Thematic Guide to Canadian Literature*, a book of literary criticism, came out in 1972, the same year as her most famous novel, *Surfacing*. She first won the Governor General's Award in 1966 for poetry with *The Circle Game*. Her children's book *Princess Prunella and the Purple Peanut* was published in 1995. She was recently awarded an honorary degree by England's Oxford University.

11 Gabrielle Roy's *The Tin Flute* was originally titled *Bonheur d'occasion* and became an award-winning film.

12 "The Cremation of Sam McGee" is by Robert Service.

13 *Who Has Seen the Wind* was written by the famous Prairie author W.O. Mitchell. Although he lived most of his life in Alberta, Mitchell was born in Weyburn, Saskatchewan.

14 "In Flanders Fields" was written by John McCrae in World War I. The doctor from Guelph, Ontario, composed the poem in 20 minutes while overlooking the grave of a fellow officer at Ypres. First published in December 1915 in *Punch* magazine, his elegy is the most famous English poem of that war.

15 Douglas Copeland invented the term "Generation X" in his book *Generation X: Tales for an Accelerated Culture*.

16 Nova Scotia native Hugh MacLennan has won the most Governor General's Awards for Literature. He is the writer who first described Canada as "two solitudes," and is the author of such novels as *Barometer Rising*, *Two Solitudes* and *The Watch That Ends the Night*. He has won the Governor General's Award five times.

17 Michael Ondaatje was born in Sri Lanka in 1943 and moved to Canada in 1962 via England. His books of poetry include *The Collected Works of Billy the Kid* (1970, Governor General's Award) and *There's a Trick with a Knife I'm Learning to Do* (1978, Governor General's Award). His novels are *Coming Through Slaughter* (1976); *Running in the Family* (1982); *In The Skin of a Lion* (1987), set in 1930s Toronto; and *The English Patient* (1992), Governor General's Award and Booker Prize winner; and most recently *Anil's Ghost*. *The English Patient* is set in Italy in World War II, and its film adaptation won the 1997 Academy Award for Best Picture.

18 Mordecai Richler (1931–2001) is the author of the popular children's book *Jacob Two-Two Meets the Hooded Fang*, published in 1975 and filmed in 1977. The story is about a little boy who gets into a lot of trouble because he always says things twice. Richler lived for a time in Paris, then London, England, before returning to Canada where he was born. His novels include *The Acrobats*, *Son of a Smaller Hero*, *The Apprenticeship of Duddy Kravitz* (filmed in 1974), *Cocksure* (1968, Governor General's Award), *St. Urbain's Horsemen* (1971, Governor General's Award), *Joshua Then and Now* (1980, filmed in 1985) and *Barney's Version*, his last novel. "No matter how long I live abroad," he wrote about the working class neighbourhood in Montreal where he grew up, "I do feel forever rooted in St. Urbain Street. That was my time, my place, and I have elected myself to get it right."

19 Sarah Binks, a fictional creation of Paul Hiebert, is perhaps Saskatchewan's best-known poet. Known as "the Sweet Songstress of Saskatchewan," Binks first came to light in 1947 in a "biography" entitled *Sarah Binks*. She is known for her exquisitely awful poetry.

20 Evangeline is the heroine and title character of Henry Wadsworth Longfellow's 1847 epic poem about the expulsion of the Acadians from Nova Scotia.

The statue of Evangeline at Grand Pré, Nova Scotia.

21 Archibald Belaney went by the name of Grey Owl, passing himself off as the son of a Scotsman and an Apache. He wrote *The Men of the Last Frontier* (1931), *Pilgrims of the Wild* (1934), *The Adventures of Sajo and Her Beaver People* (1935) and *Tales of an Empty Cabin* (1936). He twice gave a lecture tour of England and caused an uproar when his English birth was discovered on his death. Pierce Brosnan played him in a recent movie.

22 Harry Colebourn named his bear Winnipeg, or Winnie for short. When he was posted to France during World War I, he gave Winnie to the London Zoo, where she became the inspiration for A.A. Milne's famous character Winnie the Pooh.

23 In 1985 Farley Mowat was barred from entering the United States as an "undesirable." His works include *And No Birds Sang* and *A Whale for the Killing*.

24 Ernest Hemingway worked for the *Toronto Star* in the 1920s.

25 Louis Hémon, author of *Maria Chapdelaine*, was born in France in 1880.

26 Anne of Green Gables' last name is Shirley.

27 Most of the "Anne" novels were written by Lucy Maud Montgomery in Ontario. Only the original *Anne of Green Gables* was written while Montgomery still lived in Prince Edward Island.

28 Susanna Moodie wrote *Roughing It in the Bush* and *Life in the Clearings* about pioneer life.

29 The Arthur Ellis Award is an annual prize for the best Canadian crime fiction, given by The Crime Writers of Canada.

30 Orillia, Ontario, is the model for Stephen Leacock's Mariposa.

31 Anne Michaels' *Fugitive Pieces* won the 1997 Orange Prize for fiction—Britain's richest literary prize, worth £30,000. Carol Shields won it the following year for her novel *Larry's Party*.

32 Rudyard Kipling referred to Canada as "Our Lady of the Snows."

33 Leslie McFarlane was the Ontario writer responsible for many of the early Hardy Boys mystery books. McFarlane started the Hardy Boys series in 1927 under the Franklin W. Dixon pen name for publisher Edward Stratemeyer, and wrote most of the books for the next 20 years.

34 Harlequin Books, owned by the Torstar syndicate, sells 175 million copies annually in over 100 countries. It is the largest paperback publisher in the world.

35 Howard Engel is the author of the Benny Cooperman mystery series.

36 The Giller Prize is Canada's richest literary award. Winners receive $25,000 and a statuette.

37 Poet E.J. "Ned" Pratt (1883–1964), the author of "The Cachalot," "The Titanic" and "Towards the Last Spike," grew up in Newfoundland outport settlements served by his Methodist minister father. In 1904 he decided to enter the ministry himself and attended Victoria College in Toronto, where he studied theology and psychology. He was ordained in 1913 but decided to teach instead, and joined the English Department at Victoria in 1920. He published his first collection of poems, *Newfoundland Verse*, in 1923.

38 The movie version of Mordecai Richler's *The Apprenticeship of Duddy Kravitz* starred Richard Dreyfuss.

39 Earle Birney, Al Purdy and Alden Nowlan are all writers of poetry.

40 Allan Fotheringham wrote *Malice in Blunderland*.

41 Don Harron's pseudonym and alter ego is Charlie Farquharson.

42 Robertson Davies (1913–1995) wrote the Deptford Trilogy: *Fifth Business* (1970), *The Manticore* (1972, Governor General's Award) and *World of Wonders* (1975). Born at Thamesville, Ontario, Davies was educated at

Macmillan

Robertson Davies

Queen's University in Kingston and Balliol College, Oxford. He taught literature at Trinity College, University of Toronto, until 1981. His other novels include the Salterton Trilogy: *Tempest-Tost, Leaven of Malice* (1954, Leacock Medal for Humour), *A Mixture of Frailties*; and, in the 1980s, the Cornish Trilogy: *Rebel Angels, What's Bred in the Bone, The Lyre of Orpheus*; as well as *Murther and Walking Spirits* and *The Cunning Man*.

43 Playwright George Ryga authored *The Ecstasy of Rita Joe*.

44 The Stephen Leacock Medal for Humour is presented annually to the best Canadian book of humour.

45 Poet Dennis Lee wrote *Alligator Pie*.

46 Margaret Trudeau's autobiography came out in the two volumes *Beyond Reason* and *Consequences*.

47 Marie-Claire Blais is the author of the novel *La Belle Bete*, published in English as *Mad Shadows*.

48 *You Can't Print That* is written by journalist Charles Lynch.

49 The film adaptation of Timothy Findley's *The Wars* was directed by Robin Philips.

50 Montreal publisher Georges Edouard Desbarats and his engraver William Leggo invented the halftone photo-engraving process that enabled printers to etch relief engravings, or halftones, from photographs,

reproducing the image in dots of various sizes and shapes. The first halftone was produced on October 30, 1869, in Desbarats' *Canadian Illustrated News* and was a portrait of His Royal Highness Prince Arthur.

51 *Equinox* magazine is named for the times of year when day and night are of equal length.

52 *Harrowsmith Country Life Magazine* is named after Harrowsmith, Ontario.

53 Robert Fulford became the editor of *Saturday Night* in 1969. Canada's oldest consumer magazine, *Saturday Night* was established in 1887 and has won more National Magazine Awards than any other magazine. It is now defunct.

54 *The Toronto Star* is the Canadian newspaper with the largest circulation, at around 3,469,255 copies weekly. *The Globe and Mail*, which calls itself "Canada's National Newspaper," has the widest circulation outside its home city, with about 2 million weekly.

55 Bob Edwards owned and ran *The Eye Opener* in High River and Calgary.

56 Max Aitkin, Roy Thomson and Conrad Black were given the titles Lord Beaverbrook, Lord Thomson of Fleet and Lord Black of Crossharbour, respectively.

57 The Canadian Press (CP) started operations in 1917.

58 *The Montreal Gazette* is Montreal's daily English newspaper.

59 Claude Ryan was once the editor of *Le Devoir*.

Famous 1933 Hollywood "romantic" co-star, born in Cardston, Alberta.

1 Who said, "They told me I was going to have the tallest, darkest, leading man in Hollywood"?

2 Louis Del Grande played a psychic newspaper reporter in CBC TV's *Seeing Things*. In what 1981 science-fiction movie did he blow his top?

3 Name the co-hosts of the often controversial 1960s CBC TV public affairs show *This Hour Has Seven Days*.

4 Name the impersonator who appeared on Johnny Carson's *The Tonight Show* in 1985 mimicking all 18 of the singing voices on the hit song "We Are the World."

5 What was the subject of the seven-part National Film Board (NFB) series hosted by Gwynne Dyer and aired by CBC in 1983?

6 Name the host of CBC TV's experimental late night show, *90 Minutes Live*.

7 What CBC TV investigative newsmagazine was originally hosted by Eric Malling?

8 This *Beachcombers* star also had a cooking show. Name the actor and his cooking show.

9 Once one of Canada's highest paid journalists, who was the gravel-voiced Scot on Vancouver morning TV?

10 One of Canada's most famous women, she became a co-host of a television program called *Morning Magazine*.

11 Eric Peterson starred in what ACTRA Award–winning television version of a play about a World War I hero?

12 What hit television program aired regularly after *Hockey Night in Canada* from 1954 to 1966?

13 What CBC children's entertainer was awarded the Order of Canada in 1996?

14 Who left Winnipeg for Hollywood to host the TV show *Let's Make a Deal*?

15 This actor starred in both *Bonanza* and *Battlestar Galactica* on TV.

16 What is the longest running show on Canadian TV?
A. *Front Page Challenge*
B. *Hockey Night in Canada*
C. *The National*

17 Harry Jay Smith's real name was Jay Silverheels. A Canadian Mohawk actor from Brantford, Ontario, what TV serial role did he play?

18 Before he stepped into the role of anchorman for *The National*, this person was a CBC executive.

19 Two Canadian-born actors, James Doohan and William Shatner, appeared on the original *Star Trek*. What characters did they play?

20 Name the SCTV veteran who won a Tony Award for a featured part in the musical *My Favorite Year*, and was nominated for a Tony Award for his or her role in the musical *Candide*.
A. Andrea Martin
B. Catherine O'Hara
C. Martin Short
D. Rick Moranis

21 This entertainer, TV talk-show host and actor was born and raised in Kirkland Lake, Ontario.

22 One of the most successful songs by Ottawa-born singer and songwriter Paul Anka was the theme to which TV show?
A. *Jeopardy*
B. *Hockey Night in Canada*
C. *The Tonight Show*
D. *Saturday Night Live*

23 Who created the CBC TV comedy *The Newsroom*?
A. Don McKellar
B. Paul Gross
C. Bruce McDonald
D. Ken Finkleman

24 Who was the CTV foreign correspondent killed while reporting on fighting in Lebanon?
A. Joe Schlesinger
B. Matthew Halton
C. Clark Todd
D. Henry Champ

25 Who is the host of the Vancouver-based cooking show *The Urban Peasant*?
A. Ken Kostick
B. James Barber
C. Graham Kerr

26 What former CBC Radio personality now hosts the Vancouver-based CTV morning interview show?

27 Fiddle player Don Messer, with his band the Islanders, hosted *Don Messer's Jubilee* on CBC TV (1959–73), and earlier on CBC Radio. When did *Don Messer's Jubilee* first broadcast?

Don Messer and the Islanders

28 Quebec-born actor Roy Dupuis stars in what TV action series?

29 What Edmonton-born actress is best known for her role as Claire Kincaid, assistant district attorney of New York County, on the *Law & Order* series?

30 Name the Edmonton-born actor who made his TV debut on the CBC sitcom *Leo and Me* at age 15.

31 Who played selections from his favourite albums every Sunday on CBC Radio's longest-running show?

32 This former host of CBC Radio's *Morningside* sometimes appeared on other shows in his Charlie Farquharson role.

33 This former CBC Radio personality played the character Rawhide.

34 Alan Maitland co-hosted what CBC Radio show with Michael Enright, Barbara Frum and Elizabeth Gray?

35 Who was the host of CBC Radio's *Eclectic Circus*?

36 In June 1942 the National Film Board of Canada won Canada's first Academy Award for *Churchill's Island*. A newsreel about the Battle of Britain and Winston Churchill, it was directed by Stuart Legg and won the Oscar for best documentary film. How many Academy Awards has the National Film Board won in total?

37 Three Canadian movies were classified as political propaganda by the US Justice Department in 1983. Which of these won an Oscar for best documentary short subject?

38 What Canadian was known as "the hairdresser to the stars"?

39 Which of the following Canadian performers does not have a birthday on Canada Day?
A. Pamela Anderson
B. Dan Aykroyd
C. Genevieve Bujold
D. Ian Tyson

40 Which star of romantic action and adventure films from the golden age of Hollywood died in Vancouver in 1959?
A. Douglas Fairbanks
B. Errol Flynn
C. John Barrymore
D. Ronald Colman

41 Name the Canadian duo who starred in *The Matrix*.

One of two Canadian actors in *The Matrix*.

42 What Hollywood movie producer grew up in Saint John, New Brunswick, and in 1924 co-founded Metro-Goldwyn-Mayer? His star system helped make MGM the major force in the movie business until in the early 1950s.

MGM

43 What 1973 Norman Jewison musical combined rock opera with the story of the New Testament?

44 Edmonton-born actress Rae Dawn Chong won a Genie award for her performance in this film with a prehistoric theme.

45 What is the name of Bob and Doug McKenzie's first movie?

46 This Canadian-born actress won an Academy Award in 1928 for her performance in the movie *Coquette*.

47 What Québécois filmmaker's first film, *Mouvement Perpetuel* (1949), won a prize at the Cannes Film Festival and whose most famous film is *Mon Oncle Antoine* (1971)?

48 Some of the films he has directed include *Videodrome*, *Shivers* and *Rabid*.

49 What is the name of the Canadian-born actor who played surgeon Hawkeye Pierce in the 1970 Robert Altman movie *M*A*S*H*?

50 What 1940s musical about Canada, starring Betty Grable, John Payne and Carmen Miranda, was shot completely on a studio stage, with rear-screen projections of scenes of Lake Louise, Alberta?

51 What Canadian comic is the voice behind the title character in the animated cartoon *Shrek*?

52 What Vancouver-born actor was chosen to play Anakin Skywalker in Episodes 2 and 3 of the George Lucas *Star Wars* series?

53 What Six Nations actor is well known for his role as Kicking Bird in the 1990 Kevin Costner film *Dances With Wolves*?

54 Which actor and star of numerous TV series and made-for-TV movies is often mistakenly described as Canadian because he was born in Toronto—that's Toronto, Ohio?
A. Robert Urich
B. Robert Wagner
C. Robert Conrad
D. Robert Goulet

1 Fay Wray, King Kong's "romantic interest" in the original 1933 movie. Born Vina Fay Wray in 1907 at Cardston, Alberta, Wray is best known for her role as Ann Darrow, the frightened woman caught in the paw of a colossal gorilla and carried to the top of the Empire State Building. Wray landed her first bit part in a Universal western in 1923, and in 1928, won stardom in Erich von Stroheim's *The Wedding March*. From then on she played at Paramount opposite such leading men as Gary Cooper, Ronald Colman, Fredric March and William Powell.

2 In David Cronenberg's *Scanners*, Louis Del Grande literally blew his top.

3 Patrick Watson and Laurier Lapierre co-hosted *This Hour Has Seven Days*.

4 Quebec entertainer Andre-Philippe Gagnon impersonated the entire cast of the hit song "We Are the World."

5 Gwynne Dyer hosted the NFB documentary series *War*.

6 The host of *90 Minutes Live* was Peter Gzowski.

7 *The Fifth Estate* was originally hosted by Eric Malling.

8 *Celebrity Cooks*, with Bruno Gerussi, was the name of the *Beachcombers* star's long-running cooking show.

9 Jack Webster hosted his morning TV talk show from Vancouver. He died March 2, 1999.

10 In 1971, at age 22, Margaret Trudeau became the youngest "First Lady" in the world. Six years and three children later, she walked out of her marriage and in the 1970s co-hosted the *Morning Magazine* and *Margaret* shows on CJOH Television in Ottawa.

11 *Billy Bishop Goes to War* starred Eric Peterson.

12 *The Juliette Show* pulled in huge audiences every Saturday night after *Hockey Night in Canada*. Born Juliette Augustina Sysak in Winnipeg, Manitoba, "Our Pet" Juliette made her CBC radio debut at age 15, and got her own show in 1954. She retired in 1966, but did several TV specials and had a two-year comeback with *Juliette and Friends* (1973–75).

13 With his two puppet friends Casey and Finnigan, Ernie Coombs played Mr. Dressup for over 30 years. Born in Lewiston, Maine, Coombs started his career as a puppeteer on *Mr. Rogers' Neighbourhood*. He came to Canada in 1963 and started *Mr. Dressup* a year later. He was awarded the Order of Canada in 1996. Ernie Coombs died on September 18, 2001, at age 73.

14 Winnipeger Monty Hall was the host of *Let's Make a Deal*.

15 Originally a newsreader for CBC Radio, Lorne Greene starred on TV in *Bonanza* and *Battlestar Galactica*.

16 *Hockey Night in Canada* is the longest running show on Canadian TV.

17 Jay Silverheels played the role of Tonto in *The Lone Ranger*.

18 Knowlton Nash was a CBC executive before stepping in front of the camera for *The National*.

19 Chief Engineer Scott and Captain James T. Kirk were played by Canadian-born actors James Doohan and William Shatner on the original *Star Trek* series.

20 Andrea Martin won the 1992 Tony Award as Featured Actress in a Musical for *My Favorite Year*, and was nominated for a Tony for her performance in the musical *Candide* in 1997. Born and raised in Portland, Maine, she immigrated to Toronto in the 1970s and appeared with Martin Short, Gilda Radner and Victor Garber in a now legendary production of *Godspell* before moving to the Firehall Theatre and *SCTV*.

21 Alan Thicke is from Kirkland Lake, Ontario.

22 Paul Anka wrote the theme for *The Tonight Show* starring Johnny Carson. Anka and Carson were buddies.

23 *The Newsroom* was written and directed by Ken Finkleman.

24 Clark Todd was CTV's foreign correspondent in Lebanon when he was killed in the fighting in 1983.

25 The host of *The Urban Peasant* is James Barber.

26 Vicki Gabereau is the host of the award-winning *Vicki Gabereau* show on CTV. Most Canadians feel she's a better interviewer than Oprah herself.

27 *Don Messer's Jubilee* first aired on CBC Radio in 1944. Don Messer and the Islanders recorded over 30 albums. Messer died in Halifax at age 63 on March 26, 1973.

28 Roy Dupuis from Abitibi, Quebec, stars in *Nikita*.

29 After playing assistant district attorney Claire Kincaid on *Law & Order*, Edmonton-born Jillian Hennessy is now starring as Jordan Cavanagh, a Boston medical examiner, in a new one-hour drama called *Crossing Jordan*.

30 Michael J. Fox made his debut on CBC TV's *Leo and Me*. He is better known for playing yuppie-wannabe Alex P. Keaton on *Family Ties* and Mike Flaherty, deputy mayor of New York on *Spin City*.

31 Clyde Gilmour was the host of CBC Radio's longest-running show *Gilmour's Albums*. His Sunday time slot is now filled by Stuart McLean's *The Vinyl Cafe*.

32 The alter ego of Don Harron is former host of *Morningside*, Charlie Farquharson.

33 Max Ferguson played Rawhide on CBC Radio.

34 Alan Maitland was co-host of *As It Happens* on CBC Radio.

35 The host of CBC Radio's *Eclectic Circus* was Allan McFee.

36 The National Film Board of Canada has won nine Academy Awards.

37 *If You Love This Planet* won an Oscar in 1983 despite being classified as political propaganda by the US Justice Department. Two other Canadian films, *Acid Rain* and *Requiem or Recovery: Acid from Heaven*, were also classified as propaganda by the USA in 1983.

38 Sydney Guilaroff, born in Winnipeg, was hairdresser to Joan Crawford, Lucille Ball, Bette Davis, Grace Kelly and Elizabeth Taylor.

39 Ian Tyson's birthday does not fall on Canada Day.

40 Errol Flynn died in Vancouver in 1959.

41 Keanu Reeves and Carrie Ann Moss starred in *The Matrix*.

42 Louis B. Mayer (1885–1957), the Mayer in Metro-Goldwyn-Mayer, was born Ezemiel Mayer at Vilme, Russia, came to Canada as an infant, and grew up in Saint John, New Brunswick, helping his father run a salvage and scrap business. He moved to Massachusetts in about 1900 and went into the movie theatre business. He was one of the founders of the Academy of Motion Picture Arts and Sciences with fellow Canadian Mary Pickford.

43 Norman Jewison directed *Jesus Christ Superstar* in 1973. Born July 21, 1926, in Toronto, Jewison started his career in London, England, where he wrote and acted for the BBC. After moving back to Toronto, he spent six years at the CBC before turning to feature films in the 1960s. His films include *In the Heat of the Night* (1967), *Fiddler on the Roof* (1970) and *Moonstruck* (1987).

44 *Quest For Fire* earned Rae Dawn Chong a Genie award. She's the daughter of comedy star Tommy Chong.

45 Bob and Doug McKenzie's first movie is called *Strange Brew*.

46 Mary Pickford won an Academy Award in 1928.

47 Montreal director Claude Jutra (1930–1986) started working at the National Film Board of Canada in 1956, where he made his best-known work, *Mon Oncle Antoine*. Other films include *Kamouraska*, based on the Anne Hebert novel, and *Surfacing* (1981), based on the Margaret Atwood tale. Suffering from Alzheimer's disease, Jutra drowned in 1986; his body washed up on the shore of the St. Lawrence at Cap-Santé on April 19, 1987.

48 *Videodrome*, *Shivers*, and *Rabid* are three of David Cronenberg's earlier movies.

49 Donald Sutherland, born in Saint John, New Brunswick, in 1934, was educated at the University of Toronto (engineering, drama), and went on to study acting in London. Some of Sutherland's early successes include Robert Altman's *M*A*S*H* (1970), opposite Jane Fonda in *Klute* (1971), and Dalton Trumbo's *Johnny Got His Gun* (1971). He was married to Tommy Douglas's daughter Shirley (they divorced in 1970), and is the father of actor Kiefer Sutherland.

50 *Springtime in the Rockies* was shot entirely on a studio stage in Hollywood.

51 *Saturday Night Live* veteran Mike Myers is the voice behind the title character in the animated cartoon *Shrek*.

52 Hayden Christensen from Vancouver will play Anakin Skywalker in Episodes 2 and 3 of the *Star Wars* series.

53 Graham Greene played Kicking Bird in *Dances With Wolves*. Other roles include the movies *Die Hard* and *The Green Mile*, and on TV, *The X-Files* and *The Red Green Show*.

54 Robert Urich was born in Toronto, Ohio.

3 Where can you find the world's most comprehensive collection of works by British sculptor Henry Moore?

1 What Sault Ste. Marie painter's works include *Lacing Up* and *At The Crease*?

4 Who were the members of the Group of Seven in their founding show in 1920 at the Art Gallery of Toronto?

Tom Thomson in Algonquin Park.

Confederation Life

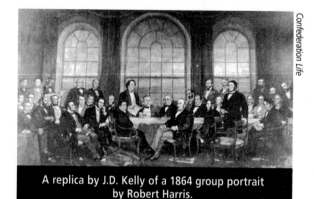

A replica by J.D. Kelly of a 1864 group portrait by Robert Harris.

2 Robert Harris painted a group portrait of the attendees at an 1864 Quebec Conference. Who were they?

5 Why was Tom Thomson, often associated with the Group of Seven, not actually a member of the group?

Death of Wolfe by Benjamin West.

6 What Canadian painter was called Klee Wyck, an Ucluelet name meaning "laughing one"?

7 American artist Benjamin West's famous painting *Death of Wolfe* is displayed at what Canadian art gallery?

8 Name the four members of the original Group of Seven artists who were born in Canada.

9 In what city can you find the Beaverbrook Art Gallery?

10 Jock MacDonald, Harold Town and a group of nine other abstract expressionists first exhibited in Toronto in 1954. Under what name did they exhibit?

11 What famous Wolfville, Nova Scotia, artist joined the Canadian Army in 1942 and served in Europe as a member of the War Art program? Two of his most well-known paintings are *Horse and Train* and *Couple on Beach*.

Royal Ontario Museum

Paul Kane, 1810–1871

12 The paintings of Paul Kane are noted for their nineteenth-century depictions of what?
A. Native life
B. Wildlife
C. Life by the sea

The 1967 Centennial silver dollar engraved by the artist of *Horse and Train* and *Couple on Beach*.

13 Before devoting himself entirely to painting, this Group of Seven member worked as an illustrator for *Harper's*. He went on to successfully create many abstract works. What is his name?

14 Canada's best-selling nature painter got his first training as a naturalist at the Royal Ontario Museum. Some of his best works have appeared on Canada Post stamps. What is his name?

15 Cornelius Krieghoff is one of Canada's best-known artists from the nineteenth century. What area of Canada did he primarily feature in his work?

16 This painter's family lost their farm in the Depression and moved to Stonewall, Manitoba, from Alberta. After leaving school he worked in lumber camps to raise money to attend art school and in the 1970s he started to write text to accompany his paintings. His book *A Prairie Boy's Winter* has become a Canadian children's classic. What is his name?

1948

17 Name the leader of a group of Montreal artists who issued the Refus Global manifesto of August 9, 1948, a declaration denouncing the traditional values and conformity of Quebec society.
A. J.W. Morrice
B. Norval Morrisseau
C. Paul-Emile Borduas
D. Gilles Tonnancourt

18 Who was the first living female artist, recently deceased, to be given a solo exhibition at the National Gallery of Canada?
A. Dorothy Knowles
B. Mary Pratt
C. Joyce Wieland
D. Daphne Odjig

19 Todd McFarlane of Calgary, Alberta, received over 700 rejections for his comic-book art before being hired in 1984 to pencil the short-lived comic *Scorpio Rose* for Marvel Comics. In 1989 he co-created Venom, which has become Marvel's most-popular villain; his *Spider-Man*, released in 1990, became the best-selling comic ever at 2.5 million copies. In early 1992, he and some other artists created the independent house Image Comics. In May 1992 Image Comics released what new series that has since become the best-selling independent comic ever, an HBO mini-series and a feature film?

20 At what location would you find Vernon March's famous war memorial sculpture?

21 In which Canadian city does the Museum of Anthropology house one of the largest collections of West Coast Native art in the world?

22 What art museum is one of the masterworks of Canadian-born architect Frank Gehry?

1 Ken Danby.

2 Robert Harris's group portrait depicted the Fathers of Confederation. The painting was destroyed in the burning of the Parliament Buildings in 1917; J.D. Kelly painted a replica for the Confederation Life Collection.

3 The Art Gallery of Ontario in Toronto houses the world's most comprehensive collection of Henry Moore sculptures.

4 The founding members of the Group of Seven were Franklin Carmichael, Lawren Harris, A.Y. Jackson, Frank Johnston, Arthur Lismer, J.E.H. MacDonald and Frederick Varley. Edwin Holgate of Quebec and Lemoyne Fitzgerald of Manitoba also joined before the group disbanded on the death of J.E.H. MacDonald in 1932. After they disbanded, members of the Group of Seven helped found the Canadian Group of Painters, which also included Emily Carr and David Milne.

5 Thomson died in a canoe accident in Algonquin Park in 1917, three years before the Group of Seven was officially formed. His canvas *The West Wind* greatly influenced the work of the Group of Seven.

6 Emily Carr (1871–1945), born in Victoria, British Columbia, was orphaned in her teens. In 1891 she studied art at the California School of Design in San Francisco; from 1899–1911 she studied in England and France, where she was influenced by impressionism, Fauvism and cubism. In 1911 she returned to Victoria to paint, supporting herself by teaching art and running a boarding house. She spent summers painting in the Queen Charlottes, grafting her own post-impressionist style onto Native imagery and coastal landscapes, with swirling forms and intense greens, blues and browns. In 1927 members of the Group of Seven painters induced the National Gallery of Canada to give her an exhibition. Carr wrote a trilogy of memoirs: *Klee Wyck* (1941) about her contacts with Aboriginal culture, *The Book of Small* (1942) on her childhood in Victoria and *The House of All Sorts* (1944) about her career as a landlady; she also wrote *Growing Pains* (1946) an account of her entire life. Her journal, *Hundreds and Thousands* (1966), was published after her death.

7 *Death of Wolfe* by Benjamin West hangs in the National Gallery of Canada, Ottawa.

8 Franklin Carmichael, Lawren Harris, A.Y. Jackson and Frank Johnston were the only original members of the Group of Seven born in Canada.

9 Fredericton, New Brunswick, is home to the Beaverbrook Art Gallery.

10 Jock MacDonald and Harold Town were members of Painters Eleven.

11 Alex Colville, born in Toronto in 1920, moved with his family to Amherst, Nova Scotia, in 1929. He studied art at Mount Allison University, Sackville, New Brunswick, and served in Europe as a war artist during World War II. At war's end, he taught art and art history at Mount Allison from 1946 to 1963, before retiring to paint full-time. Since 1973 he and his wife Rhoda have lived in Wolfville, Nova Scotia, in the house where Rhoda was born.

12 Paul Kane's paintings are known for their depictions of the lives of First Nations people in the nineteenth century, mainly in the West. In February 2002, his painting of British surveyor John Henry Lefroy, *Scene in*

the Northwest—Portrait (1845–1846), sold at auction for a record $4.6 million—$5,062,500 with the buyer's premium added—making it the most valuable painting in Canadian history.

13 Lawren Harris (1885–1970) was born in Brantford, Ontario, into the family that co-owned the Massey-Harris farm machinery company. Harris attended the University of Toronto for a year, then studied art in Europe, returning to Canada in 1908. He began painting Toronto houses in the immigrant district, and in 1914 helped plan and finance the Studio Building on Severn Street in Toronto as a workshop for Canadian painters such as A.Y. Jackson, Tom Thomson, J.E.H. MacDonald, Franklin Carmichael and Harris himself. In his later career he began experimenting with abstract works.

14 Robert Bateman, born in Toronto in 1930, is Canada's best-selling nature painter. In the 1950s and 1960s, Bateman taught high-school geography and art in Toronto and Burlington, but after seeing an Andrew Wyeth exhibition in 1963, he began to paint the realistic wildlife subjects that have made him famous.

15 Krieghoff paintings focused on the *habitants* of mid-nineteenth-century Quebec. Born in Amsterdam in 1815, he is best known for his hundreds of portraits, sporting scenes and narrative paintings of Quebec *habitant* life. He and his brother Ernst emigrated to America in 1835 and fought for the US army in the Seminole War in Florida. He met Louise Gauthier from Boucherville, Quebec, in New York and moved with her to Montreal in 1840. After a year studying in Paris, he moved to Longueuil village across the St. Lawrence from Montreal, but also kept a studio in the city. In

NLC

A Native chief by Paul Kane.

1853, auctioneer John Budden persuaded him to move to Quebec, where his canvases were popular with lumber merchants and army officers.

16 William Kurelek (1927–1977) was born on his family's homestead near Whitford, Alberta, the eldest of seven children. He is best known for creating *A Prairie Boy's Winter*. Kurelek also painted religious art, which helped him cope with his frequent depressions. He died in Toronto on November 3, 1977. Some of his works, including *The Canadian Pioneer* and *The Passion of Christ*, can be seen in Niagara Falls.

17 Paul-Emile Borduas (1905–1960) was the leader of the Mouvement Automatiste and in 1948 helped draw up the Refus Global manifesto, which demanded freedom of expression and denounced the suffocating nature of Quebec society. Born in St-Hilaire, Quebec, he was encouraged by Ozias Leduc to study at the École des beaux-arts in Montreal (1923–27) and in Paris (1928–30) at the Ateliers d'art sacré. In 1937 he started teaching at the École du Meuble in Montreal, but moved to New York in 1953, then to Paris until 1960.

18 Joyce Wieland's exhibition *True Patriot Love*, 1971, was the first solo exhibition at the National Gallery of Canada by a living female artist.

19 Todd McFarlane is the creator of *Spawn*, first released as a comic series by Image Comics in 1992. Born March 16, 1961, in Calgary, Alberta, Todd started illustrating his own comic books in high school, but his first passion was baseball. While attending Washington State University on a baseball scholarship he broke his ankle sliding into home plate, which ended his dreams of having a pro career.

20 The famous war memorial sculpture by Vernon March is at Confederation Square, Ottawa.

21 The Museum of Anthropology at the University of British Columbia in Vancouver houses one of the largest collections of West Coast Native art in the world.

22 The Guggenheim Museum in Bilbao, Spain, one of the most famous buildings in the world, is the work of Canadian-born architect Frank Gehry.

Museo Guggenheim Bilbao

The Guggenheim Museum in Bilbao, Spain.

CANADA PERFORMS

A scene from *Le Théâtre de Neptune*.

1 When and where was *Le Théâtre de Neptune*, Canada's first play, performed?

2 In which city can you find today's Neptune Theatre?

3 Niagara-on-the-Lake in Ontario is the site of a theatre festival devoted to which playwright?

4 The Stratford Festival was established by the director who went on in 1960 to establish the National Theatre School in Montreal, Canada's first theatre school. When was the Stratford Festival founded and by whom?

5 Where is the Confederation Centre of the Arts, opened in 1964?

6 What Metis military leader starred in Buffalo Bill's Wild West Show?

7 This popular baritone made his Broadway debut in the 1961 production of *Camelot*.

8 What was the name of the popular World War I vaudeville troupe formed by Canadian Army soldiers that became the first Canadian musical act on Broadway?
A. Happy Gang
B. Dumbells
C. Air Farce
D. Wobblies

9 Where is the Rainbow Stage?

10 Eric Peterson was given rave reviews for his role in a play about a World War I flying ace. What was the name of the play?

11 Where in Canada is the Citadel Theatre?

12 What was the home province of the Mummers Troupe?

The first Canadian musical act on Broadway.

13 What folksinger from Ottawa played the part of Hank Williams in *Hank Williams: The Show He Never Gave*?

14 What playwright's works include *Les Belles Soeurs* and *Hosanna*?

15 Who was a founder of the Manitoba Theatre Centre and later appointed artistic director of the Stratford Festival?

16 In what city are there theatres named 25th Street and Persephone?

17 Who is the Calgary author of the play *Blood Relations*?

18 In which city will you find the Factory Theatre and the Firehall Theatre?

19 What small theatre in Montreal's Place des Arts is named after the father of a famous separatist?

20 Who wrote the music to "O Canada"?

21 What Canadian recording artist has won the most Grammy Awards?
A. Céline Dion
B. Oscar Peterson
C. "Polka King" Walter Ostanek
D. Alanis Morissette

22 Name the wealthy composer who in 1982 was outbid by Toronto's Honest Ed Mirvish in the purchase of London, England's famous Old Vic Theatre?

23 The French folk song "Alouette" is about what kind of bird?

24 Which virtuoso violinist and conductor was named music director of the National Arts Centre Orchestra in Ottawa in 1997?
A. Itzhak Perlman
B. Pinchas Zukerman
C. Yehudi Menuhin
D. Yo-Yo Ma

Cdn. Enclylopedia

Composer of "Swinging Shepherd Blues."

25 What flute and saxophone virtuoso's biggest hit was "Swinging Shepherd Blues"?

26 Elmer Iseler founded and directed the Festival Singers of Canada and the Elmer Iseler Singers and was the conductor of the Toronto Mendelssohn Choir for 33 years. He also took a chance on an unknown Canadian brass quintet, taking them on their first European tour in 1972. What was the name of the quintet?

27 What is the home city of the Bach Choir?

28 With what instrument is the name Ofra Harnoy associated?

29 Who is called Canada's first lady of the classical guitar?

Famous Canadian pianist performing in 1957.

30 This famed Canadian pianist died in 1982 at the age of 50.

31 What type of performance do you associate with the name Teresa Stratas?

32 Name the Quebec composer who scored the musical *Notre Dame de Paris*.

33 What was the name of Guy Lombardo's band?

34 What baritone caused a controversy in 1978 by inserting the line "We stand on guard for rights and liberty" in a rendition of the national anthem at the Montreal Forum?

35 Where was Canada's first ballet company established?

36 After dancing *Giselle*, *Swan Lake*, *The Nutcracker*, *Romeo and Juliet*, *La Sylphide* and scores of other ballets, this dancer wrote a 1994 autobiography, *Movement Never Lies*.

163

1 Canada's first play, *Le Théâtre de Neptune* by Marc Lescarbot, was performed at Port Royal, Nova Scotia, on November 14, 1606. It was staged in canoes outside the fort, complete with verses in French, Gascon and Mi'kmaq. The play was a "jovial spectacle" in which King Neptune arrived in a floating chariot drawn by six Tritons, to the sound of trumpets and cannons, to greet Samuel de Champlain as he returned to Port-Royal with Jean de Biencourt de Poutrincourt, the governor of Acadia.

2 The Neptune Theatre is in Halifax, Nova Scotia.

3 The Shaw Festival at Niagara-on-the-Lake is the only festival in the world specializing in the plays of George Bernard Shaw and his contemporaries (1856–1950). CBC producer Andrew Allan (1907–1974) was founding artistic director of the Festival, followed by Paxton Whitehead and Christopher Newton. The Shaw started operations in the town's old courthouse in 1962 with a production of *Man and Superman*, and moved to a new Festival Theatre in 1973. In 1980 the Festival acquired the Royal George Theatre and started a tradition of operating three theatres, each with its own type of play.

4 In 1951, Tom Patterson (b. 1920) approached the Stratford city council to start a summer Shakespearean festival. The first season of the Stratford Festival opened in a tent in 1953, with Tyrone Guthrie (1900–1971) as artistic director.

5 Charlottetown, Prince Edward Island, is home to the Confederation Centre of the Arts.

6 Gabriel Dumont was a star in Buffalo Bill's Wild West Show.

7 Robert Goulet was born in Lawrence, Massachusetts, of French-Canadian ancestry. Brought up in Edmonton, he won a singing scholarship to the Royal Conservatory of Music in Toronto and, in 1951, made his concert debut in Edmonton in Handel's *Messiah*. He sang with the Canadian Opera Company and at the Stratford Festival before landing the role of Lancelot in Lerner and Loewe's Broadway premiere of *Camelot* in 1960 opposite Richard Burton and Julie Andrews. He won the 1962 Grammy for Best New Artist. Robert Goulet's hit songs include "On a Clear Day You Can See Forever," "My Love Forgive Me" and "Camelot" and he has appeared in numerous movies.

8 The Canadian Army vaudeville troupe The Dumbells first performed at Vimy Ridge in 1917 and premiered their musical review in London in 1919. They followed up with rave reviews at the Grand Theatre in Toronto and opened a new variety show at the Ambassador Theatre in New York two years later, becoming the first Canadian musical act on Broadway. The Dumbells disbanded in 1929.

9 The Rainbow Stage is in Winnipeg, Manitoba. When the flood of 1950 washed away the original bandstand at Kildonan Municipal Park, it was replaced by the Rainbow Stage Theatre, completed in 1952.

10 *Billy Bishop Goes to War*, written by John Gray and Eric Peterson, starred Eric Peterson and toured Canada in 1978, getting rave reviews. It opened on Broadway in 1980 and won the Governor General's Award for Drama in 1983.

11 The Citadel Theatre started life in Edmonton in November 1965, when 300 people crowded into the tiny Salvation Army Citadel to watch a performance of *Who's Afraid of Virginia Woolf?* By the end of that first year, 1,300 citizens had subscribed to the Citadel's second season.

12 The Mummers Troupe was founded in Newfoundland.

13 Sneezy Waters starred in *Hank Williams: The Show He Never Gave*.

14 Quebec playwright Michel Tremblay (1942–) wrote *Les Belles Soeurs* and *Hosanna* in 1968 and 1970. The plays shocked many in Quebec because of their free artistic use of raw French street slang—*joual*. Bill Glassco, founder of the Tarragon Theatre in Toronto, first staged the works of Tremblay in English.

15 John Hirsch co-founded Canada's oldest English-language regional theatre, the Manitoba Theatre Centre, in 1957 with Tom Hendry. In 1981 he became artistic director of the Stratford Festival.

16 Both the 25th Street Theatre, founded in 1972 by students of the University of Saskatchewan drama department, and the Persephone Theatre, founded in 1974 by Brian Richmond and Janet and Susan Wright, are in Saskatoon, Saskatchewan.

17 *Blood Relations* was written by Calgary playwright Sharon Pollock. Born Mary Sharon Chalmers in Fredericton, Pollock's plays have been produced at the Stratford Festival and across Canada. Two of her plays, *Blood Relations* and *Doc*, have won the Governor General's Award. In 1989 she appeared in her own play, *Getting It Straight*, at the International Women's Festival in Winnipeg. She also directs, and recently staged Harold Pinter's *Betrayal* in Calgary. Other plays include *One Tiger to a Hill*, *Whiskey Six Cadenza*, *Moving Pictures*, *End Dream* and *Angel's Trumpet*.

18 Toronto is home to the Factory Theatre and the Firehall Theatre.

19 Théâtre Jean Duceppe in Montreal's Place des Arts is named in honour of the father of Bloc Quebecois leader Gilles Duceppe.

20 "O Canada" was composed in 1880 by Calixa Lavallée, with French lyrics by A.B. Routhier, for the St-Jean-Baptiste celebration; a 1908 English version was written by Stanley Weir.

CANADA PERFORMS

21 Jazz pianist Oscar Peterson is the Canadian with the most Grammy awards—seven Grammies and eleven nominations. In 1972 he became an Officer of the Order of Canada.

22 Andrew Lloyd Webber, composer of *Cats*, was outbid by Honest Ed Mirvish in his attempt to purchase the Old Vic Theatre in London.

23 The bird in the song "Alouette" is a lark.

24 Pinchas Zukerman became the music director of the National Arts Centre Orchestra in 1997.

25 Jazz great Moe Koffman's best-known hit is "Swinging Shepherd Blues."

26 The Canadian Brass was discovered by Elmer Iseler in 1972.

27 The Bach Choir is based in Montreal.

28 Ofra Harnoy plays the cello.

29 Liona Boyd is Canada's first lady of the classical guitar. Boyd was born in London, England, in 1949, came to Canada at age 6, and became a Canadian citizen in 1975. She rose to prominence in 1976 when she toured North America with Gordon Lightfoot. To bring classical guitar to a wider audience, she has performed with Tracy Chapman, Georges Zamphir, Roger Whitaker, Eric Clapton and Chet Atkins, and as a soloist and with symphony orchestras.

Toronto Telegram

Glenn Gould in the 1950s.

30 Glenn Gould (1932–1982) was born in Toronto, studied at the Royal Conservatory of Music and soloed with the Toronto Symphony at age 14. His brilliant 1955 recording of Bach's *Goldberg Variations* won him instant global acclaim. He toured in Europe and the USA, and from 1961 to 1964 co-directed the summer music program at Stratford, but he disliked public life and in 1964 retired from the stage, preferring to record in the studio. His contrapuntal clarity and unorthodox performances of Bach and Beethoven as well as Schoenberg and Hindemith became well known. He did CBC TV and radio documentaries and wrote for magazines and newspapers. He died of a massive stroke on October 4, 1982, apparently due to complications from medication, at age 50.

31 Soprano Teresa Stratas is an opera singer. She has performed around the world, including at the Metropolitan in New York and La Scala in Milan.

NLC

32 The musical *Notre Dame de Paris* was composed by Luc Plamondon.

33 Guy Lombardo's band was called The Royal Canadians.

34 Roger Doucet, who sang "O Canada" at the home games of the Montreal Canadiens, inserted the line "We stand on guard for rights and liberty," causing a minor controversy in 1978.

35 Canada's first ballet company was the Royal Winnipeg Ballet company, established in Winnipeg in 1938 by Gwyneth Lloyd and Betty Hall.

36 Karen Kain is one of Canada's greatest ballet dancers. Her autobiography *Movement Never Lies* was published in 1994. She was inspired to study ballet as a girl when she saw Celia Franca, the founding director of the National Ballet of Canada, perform in *Giselle* at Hamilton's Palace Theatre in 1959. In 1973, she and Frank Augustyn went to the Moscow International Ballet Festival and took top honours in duet ensemble work for their performance of the Bluebird pas de deux from *Sleeping Beauty*. In the fall of 1994, her 25th anniversary year with the National Ballet of Canada, Kain gave her final performance of *Swan Lake*.

1 What Canadian made over 350 films, directed Charlie Chaplin, W.C. Fields and Buster Keaton, and was awarded a special Oscar in 1937—"to the master of fun, discoverer of stars ... for his lasting contribution to the comedy technique of the screen"?

3 Dave Broadfoot sometimes plays Sergeant Renfrew on the *Royal Canadian Air Farce*, having been a former member of comedy troupe. Who are the members of *The Royal Canadian Air Farce*?

6 What former press secretary to Pierre Trudeau had a short-lived stint as a newscaster on the Global network, but her son Matthew went on to a lucrative career with the cast of the TV sitcom *Friends*?

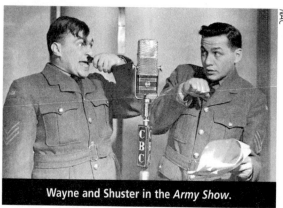

NAC

Wayne and Shuster in the *Army Show*.

4 Who is the author of the comic strip *For Better or For Worse*?

5 John Candy played Johnny La Rue on the SCTV Network. Who played Count Floyd and Sammy Maudlin?

7 What Canadian talk show's logo button was worn by Robin Williams while playing Mork?

2 On what show did the Canadian comedy team Johnny Wayne and Frank Shuster make more appearances than any other guest?
A. *Front Page Challenge*
B. *The Ed Sullivan Show*
C. *Your Show of Shows*
D. *Tommy Hunter*

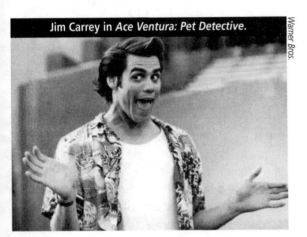
Jim Carrey in *Ace Ventura: Pet Detective.*

Warner Bros.

10
What Toronto-born impresario is creator and executive producer of the show *Saturday Night Live*?

11 This Kingston, Ontario, comedian is best known as one of the Blues Brothers.

Dreamworks
Tom Green in *Road Trip.*

8 What form of entertainment was Jim Carrey known for at the start of his career?
A. Acrobatics
B. Impersonations
C. Singing
D. Stand-up comedy

9 In the early 1980s, Toronto comic Dave Foley met Kevin McDonald at an improv class and they started working as a comedy team while employed as movie ushers. In 1984 they merged with another team— Bruce McCulloch, Mark McKinney and Scott Thompson—to form The Kids in the Hall troupe. Their sketch comedy TV show appeared on HBO, Comedy Central, CBS and the CBC over several years. What was the name of the motion picture they released in 1996?

12 Of the following famous Canadians, which one has not been a guest star on *The Simpsons*?
A. Phil Hartman
B. Donald Sutherland
C. Jim Carrey
D. Alex Trebek

13 Tom Green painted his parents' car with a lesbian scene, taped himself to street-light poles while throwing pitas, released an album titled *Huh, stiffenin against the wall* with his high school band, Organized Rhyme, and for a time, had a radio show on CHUO at what Canadian university?

1 Mack Sennett was born in Richmond, Quebec, and at age 17 moved with his parents to the USA. In 1912 he and two bookies formed the Keystone production company, featuring actors "Fatty" Arbuckle and Charles Chaplin. In 1914 alone, Sennett directed Chaplin in 35 comedies. In 1915 he, D.W. Griffith and Thomas Ince founded Triangle Films and started producing more tightly scripted films with stars such as Bobby Vernon and Gloria Swanson, and in 1917 he formed Mack Sennett Comedies. When the Depression hit, he went to Paramount and produced shorts featuring W.C. Fields as well as Bing Crosby musicals. But by 1935 he was broke and returned to Canada a pauper.

Wayne & Shuster (CBC)

2 Wayne and Shuster made more appearances on *The Ed Sullivan Show* than any other guest. They started performing for the *Army Show* in World War II, and in 1946 got their own CBC radio program. They made the transition to TV and became regulars on *The Ed Sullivan Show*, appearing 67 times. Wayne and Shuster were twice chosen by TV critics and editors in the USA as the best comedy team in North America. Wayne passed away in 1990, Shuster in 2002.

3 *The Royal Canadian Air Farce* is Roger Abbot, Don Ferguson, Luba Goy and John Morgan.

4 Lynn Johnson. On September 9, 1979, Corbeil, Ontario's Lynn Johnson premiered her *For Better or For Worse* cartoon strip in selected newspapers; two years later, she had 50 million readers worldwide in over 1,600 newspapers in the USA, Canada and 21 other countries. Based on her own family life, the strip was originally produced from a lakeside cabin in Northern Ontario. In 1985 she won the Reuben Award for Outstanding Cartoonist of the Year (first woman to win this award) from the US National Cartoonists Society (NCS) and Best Syndicated Comic Strip from the NCS in 1992.

5 Joe Flaherty played Count Floyd and Sammy Maudlin for *SCTV*.

6 Suzanne Perry, Matthew Perry's mother, was a former press secretary to Pierre Trudeau.

7 Robin Williams' character wore a *Canada After Dark* button in the TV sitcom *Mork and Mindy*.

8 Jim Carrey started his career doing impersonations.

9 In 1996, The Kids in the Hall released the movie *Brain Candy*.

10 Lorne Michaels, creator and executive producer of *Saturday Night Live*, was born in Toronto.

11 Dan Aykroyd is from Kingston, Ontario.

12 Jim Carrey has not guest-starred on *The Simpsons*—not yet, anyway. However, in a story set in the year 2010, an adult Lisa Simpson and her boyfriend go to a Jim Carrey film festival featuring "40 classic films."

13 Tom Green has built a career on outrageous antics of questionable taste. After hosting a show at the University of Ottawa on CHUO Radio, he launched *The Tom Green Show* in 1994 on Rogers Community Cable, where he built up a large following. Within two years he moved to the Canadian Comedy Network, and then onto MTV in the USA, where he became a superstar. He has been romantically linked to Drew Barrymore and even Monica Lewinsky.